THE
TEARS
OF MY
SOUL

THE
TEARS
OF MY
SOUL

Kim Hyun Hee

WILLIAM MORROW AND COMPANY, INC. / NEW YORK

It is the policy of William Morrow and Company, Inc., and its imprints and affiliates, recognizing the importance of preserving what has been written, to print the books we publish on acid-free paper, and we exert our best efforts to that end.

Library of Congress Cataloging-in-Publication Data

Kim, Hyŏn-hŭi.
  The tears of my soul / by Kim Hyun-Hee.
     p.   cm.
  1. Kim, Hyŏn-hŭi.   2. Terrorists—Korea (North)—Biography.
  3. KAL Flight 858 Bombing Incident, 1987.   I. Title.
  ISBN 0-688-12833-5
  HV6248.K516A3   1993
  364.1'092—dc20
  [B]   93-9362
                                                                            CIP

Printed in the United States of America

First Edition

1 2 3 4 5 6 7 8 9 10

THIS BOOK IS dedicated to the families of the
victims of Flight 858.
All proceeds deriving from the
book will be donated to them.

THE
TEARS
OF MY
SOUL

PROLOGUE

April 26, 1989. Seoul, South Korea.

I sat in the drab and gloomy defendant's waiting room with a choking feeling, awaiting my sentencing. Outside, in the hall that led to the courtroom, the angry crowd surged against the door, and for a moment I was afraid they would break it down. Their voices swelled in a hideous roar, and the whole building seemed to shake with their curses.

Murderer, murderer, murderer . . .

I clenched my hands and felt my whole body shudder. They were yelling about me.

No. They were yelling *at* me.

As I trembled listening to their screams, I thought of the treason trials in the People's Court right after Korea's liberation from Japan that we had learned about in school. I could now feel how terrifying they must have been to the people involved.

Though there were others in the room—a doctor, a nurse, and three special agents who had all but lived with me this past year—I had never felt more alone. It didn't matter how close I felt to these people, or they to me; it was I, not they, who was to be sentenced. At that moment how I envied them their innocence, and their future, and I felt a pang of grief rush through me.

I tried to recall the comforting Bible verses that the minister had written down for me earlier, but my thoughts were interrupted as the door opened and four policemen with starched uniforms and shiny badges arrived to escort me to the courtroom. Surrounding me protectively, they pushed their way through the angry, milling crowd and led me inside. At once the spectators erupted. This was my first appearance before the public, who'd been prohibited from watching the trial itself but were being allowed to witness the sentencing. They shouted insults and curses like hungry, ferocious animals. Had they been permitted, they would gladly have torn me limb from limb.

"Fucking bitch," an old woman hissed at me from the spectators' area. "You murdered my only son. Who will take care of me now?"

My walk forward to the defendant's box seemed to go on forever; and when at last I was able to sit down, I could no longer maintain my composure. My heart was racing, and my body shook all out of control. I began to cry, and whispered one word to myself over and over: *Mother.*

Of all the fates she might have imagined for her daughter, this was one she never could have conceived. She had raised me with endless kindness and utter devotion; and all I could think was that I had failed her. I remembered, at that moment, the way she used to fuss over me and dress me in my school uniforms and how she adorned them with laces she'd made herself. To see me now would have broken her heart.

But there was something even worse. I had failed not only her, I had failed my country as well. My confession to the South Korean authorities had to be regarded by my government as the worst possible treason. Because of my failure, and because of my disgrace, my family would almost certainly be taken from their homes and interred by the North Korean government in some horrible slave labor camp, probably for the rest of their lives. I had not only ruined my own life, I had also irrevocably ruined theirs.

The droning court proceedings began, but I could not focus on them. It seemed to me a foregone conclusion that I would be sentenced to death. I had sabotaged Korean Air Flight 858; I was responsible for the deaths of 115 people. Strangely, though, it was not until I walked into that highly charged courtroom that the impact, the full horror, of what I'd done really hit me. Though I'd hidden a bomb aboard the plane, I had seen neither the explosion nor the crash site, and until now had felt an odd sense of removal from my crime, as if it hadn't happened, or it wasn't really my fault. But being made to confront the victims' grieving families here in this courtroom, I finally began to feel, deep down, the sheer horror of the atrocity I'd committed. I could not bring myself to look toward the spectators. Each one of them was a life that I had ruined. I felt too weak; I didn't have the courage.

Causing me the most agony were the few, mostly old women, who were still clinging to the hope that the whole incident had been a hoax, and that their family members had been hidden away somewhere by the South Korean government and were still alive.

I cried even harder. I wanted to reach out to them and hold them all and tell them how truly sorry I was.

When I had set out on my mission, some two years earlier, I had been told that I was doing my country the highest possible service. I had believed unquestioningly in Our Great Leader, Kim Il Sung, as the savior of North Korea. But I knew now how incredibly naive I had been to believe such things. I had not brought about the unification of Korea, as Kim's operatives had said I would. I was no national heroine, as they had promised I'd be. What I was, in fact, was someone less than human; I was worthless, a contemptible monster.

With a start I realized that I was holding the minister's Bible verses in my hand. I could not read them through my tears, but somehow I recalled the words:

Do not fear, for I am with you;
Do not be dismayed, for I am your God.
I will strengthen you and help you;
I will uphold you with my righteous hand.

Saying these words to myself did not comfort me. I could not believe that any God, no matter how benevolent, could forgive me for what I had done.

During the long months of my internment my one consolation was that I would soon be permitted to die. I had already cheated death once: When my fellow conspirator Kim Seung Il and I were arrested in the Bahrain airport, we had each, per our orders, tried to commit suicide by biting into the cyanide ampules that had been planted in our cigarettes. Mr. Kim succeeded, dying instantly; but somehow I was revived and brought back from death to endure, alone, month after month, the guilt and pain of my crime and the grief it had caused. It was fitting, I thought, that I, the younger agent, should live a while longer and suffer.

Suddenly I was asked to stand, and I realized that at last I was to be sentenced. The judge asked if I had anything to say before he imposed the sentence. I tried to calm myself and finally managed to stammer haltingly:

"I have at last realized the gravity of my crime. I am thankful that I have had the chance to tell the truth and to learn the truth as well. I feel nothing but hatred toward Kim Il Sung, and I feel utterly inadequate to offer my apology to the families of the victims." I paused, trying to gather the courage to ask for mercy. For although I knew that I deserved death, and for months had welcomed the thought of it, I began to quail at the prospect now that it was so much closer, so much more real. But I could not manage to say another word; I found myself swallowing the words and keeping silent, while rationalizing to myself that staying alive would be worse than dying, that begging for mercy would be petty and dishonorable. And yet some instinct in me kept stirring in the back of my mind, pushing me to speak. Suddenly I had this strange feeling that there was something I needed to do, some task or penance that needed to be performed. I had to stay alive, I had to . . .

But the judge droned on, interpreting my silence as final, and I found myself hearing the words "Having received the order from Kim Jung Il, the son of Kim Il Sung, to destroy by explosive device the Korean Air Flight 858, and having carried out the said order, thereby killing one hundred and fifteen innocent lives . . . In order to express our utmost desire to deter such behavior, this court chooses the maximum penalty. The death penalty is hereby imposed."

A roar erupted from the crowd. And though this was the

10

sentence I had expected, I suddenly felt light-headed, and my stomach seemed to fall away. The blood chilled in my veins, and for a moment I froze, as tears again sprang to my eyes.

Farewell, Mother and Father, and Sister Hyun Ok and Brother Hyun Soo. I am lost to you now, at last.

I was led from the courtroom, so shaken that I was mercifully oblivious to the taunts and screams that were hurled after me. On the prison transport bus I feverishly wished with all my heart that I could see my family just once before I died, knowing all the while that such a hope was futile. I thought of my mischievous brother and beautiful sister and prayed that they would take better care of themselves and not end up like me. And I thought again how merciless the North Korean government would be toward them. Regardless of the fact that my family had been completely ignorant of my mission (indeed they had never even known that I had become a spy in the first place), they, too, would be made to pay a terrible price for my confession, for my betrayal of my country.

I was in agony. The only thing I could do now was to begin counting; yes, counting the days until they would kill me.

CHAPTER ONE

WHEN I THINK of the millions of babies born in North Korea every year, and also think back to all the babies born there in the past forty years, since the liberation from Japan, I feel a sense of outrage. Each child was, and will be, taught exactly the same things that I was, and will believe the same lies. What a terrible waste of human life that this is allowed to happen. It also somewhat explains how I became motivated to do what I did.

I was born on January 27, 1962. Because I was my mother's first child, everyone, and especially my grandparents, were all hoping for a boy. Naturally when I emerged from the womb, they were disappointed.

I was born at my maternal grandparents' house in Gaesung. My father was away at the time, so my grandparents helped to care for me. Their disappointment soon faded; my mother would later tell me that they all loved me right away and treated me like a precious doll.

My father had an important job in the Department of Foreign Affairs, about which the rest of my family knew little. When he returned from his overseas assignment and saw me for the first time, he treated me with the same reverence and kindliness as my grandparents, and he continued to do so until four years ago, the last time we saw each other.

By South Korean standards we could barely have been called middle-class, but for North Koreans we considered ourselves privileged. It was a luxury, for example, to always have cooking oil in the house and to be able to fry food. I would later learn that cooking oil was very common in the South, and that everyone could fry food.

We lived in the North Korean capital of Pyongyang in a small apartment that we felt lucky to own ourselves. Most people at my father's high level were granted their own residences, but among the working class it was common for families to share apartments and for as many as ten families to use a single bathroom.

About a year after my birth my father was posted to Cuba, and I spent the next several years living down the street from the North Korean embassy in Havana. The government of Fidel Castro had only recently installed him as president, and although the political climate was still somewhat chaotic, Cuba was far more prosperous than North Korea. We lived with other embassy families in an enormous mansion that had belonged to a bourgeois family before the revolution. The house had been stripped down and remodeled, because it had once contained many expensive sculptures and other fancy ornaments, such as crystal chandeliers and gilt-framed furniture. These had been disposed of to cleanse it of all bourgeois trappings.

Cuba in those days was much freer than North Korea, and we actually felt ourselves reasonably well off. My mother would later tell me that she considered our time in Cuba to be the best period of her life. She loved to go shopping in the supermarkets, where the sheer variety of food was astonishing to us. Not knowing any better, I assumed that children everywhere lived like this.

At noon every day an ice-cream truck would pass by the compound, and I would run to it with a few coins yelling, *"Heladero! Heladero!"* (Ice cream man! Ice cream man!) My mother nicknamed me the Chocolate General because of my fanatic love for chocolate.

We frequently attended diplomatic dinners, and I was very curious about the black- and white-skinned foreigners. I was especially struck by the blond-haired guests, who seemed so alien and exotic. I in turn was admired and cuddled by our embassy's Cuban secretaries, who were always taking me on their laps.

There was a piano on the first floor of our mansion, and every day my mother gave me a lesson. She had learned to play as a child and was quite talented. Later on, when we returned to North Korea, I found that for an ordinarily family to have a piano in their house was unthinkable. Only someone who'd been permitted to train to become a professional might have one.

Our days in Cuba blended together in a happy, dreamlike quality. I often played with other children, the most unforgettable of whom was the son of Ambassador Kim Jae Bong. He used to beat me up just for the fun of it and was always tormenting me about something. He destroyed my rubber raft, a treasured birthday present, by puncturing it with his chopsticks. And whenever I tried to ignore him, he would stand outside our house and yell, "Hyun Hee, play with me!" He was like a cat; he would repeat this call a hundred times until at last I gave in and came outside.

Interestingly I encountered him years later in North Korea, when I was in middle school. We noticed each other on the street one day, and before I could react, he gave me an embarrassed look and walked away. I knew he recognized me, and it gave me some consolation that he remembered what a menace he had been!

One of my fondest memories of this period was one day finding the door to the roof unlocked. I took my younger sister, Hyun Ok, and several other children up there to play. We sat there for hours, dangling our feet over the edge and gazing across the rooftops into the distance. Eventually some Cuban maintenance workers spotted us and informed our parents, who rushed up, white-faced, to shepherd us to safety.

Even in those halcyon days we were inculcated with the doctrines of Kim Il Sung. The first words we learned were "Thank you, Kim Il Sung, Our Great Leader." We were taught to feel hatred at the word *America,* and even among young children anti-American sentiment ran deep. In North Korea they refer to America as "the eternal enemy with whom we can never coexist under the same sky." During our stay in Cuba my father often spoke of the "imminent attack by the Yankee Imperialists." And once, when we were at the beach (which was like a magical world to me, with the endless sand and water), he pointed to some land that was barely visible on the horizon. "That's America, Hyun Hee, the worst place in the world." His words frightened me, and I became afraid that my rubber raft might slip away and be carried off to America. I also became frightened at the empty bottles and cans that drifted ashore, which I was told came from America. After that I was too frightened even to return to the beach.

We stayed in Cuba for five years before my father was recalled to Pyongyang, and during that time a brother, Hyun Soo, was born. Before we left, my mother took me to get my hair permed, saying that in North Korea it would be impossible to have it done. I wasn't to know it at the time, but my life was about to change forever.

When we returned to Pyongyang, I was enrolled in Hashin Public Elementary School. It was here that our ideological training began in earnest. Academic studies, in fact, took up less than half of our time. During the bulk of the day we were kept busy learning about the life of Our Great Leader, Kim Il Sung. We were taught a song called "Pumpkin Head," about Kim Il Sung's defeat of the Japanese years earlier. He was said to have beaten them so badly that the Japanese soldiers had been unable to carry their corpses home and could only bring the heads. All students were enrolled in extracurricular activities with an ideological bent, and these were so intensive that we would often not come home until ten at night.

During the winter of my third year ten of us were chosen to sing at a youth festival, which we were told would be attended by Kim Il Sung himself. For two months we rehearsed our song, which was entitled, "We Love the Uniform Which Our Great Leader Gave Us." During this period, when the rehearsals had ended, I was forced to wait for the late bus, sometimes for hours, and my feet ended up freezing. And during the practice sessions, though I longed for home, I never complained, knowing that it was a great honor to sing for Our Beloved Leader.

That year there was a great flood, which made it necessary for all the ground-floor families in our apartment building to move upstairs and share our homes. For the children this was great fun, and we would spend our nights on the rooftop watching the water level gradually recede.

Shortly after the flood there were terrible rumors about a possible outbreak of war with America, stemming from the sinking of the U.S.S. *Pueblo*. The atmosphere in Pyongyang became tense, and families began to pack food and clothes as they prepared to evacuate the city. Posters were placed all over the streets with the slogan CONFRONTATION WILL BE MET WITH CONFRONTATION; RETALIATION WITH RETALIATION. The adults, preparing for the impending war, worked to exhaustion, but for the children it was great fun. We would steal food that had been stockpiled and watch the proceedings with great interest. Sometimes, late at night, the blackout sirens would wake us, and we would proceed to the roof and watch Pyongyang go black. On other nights, usually around four A.M., the air-raid sirens would go off, and we would clamber out of bed and run to the nearby hill where the bomb shelter was.

During this period two of Kim Il Sung's close advisers, Ho Bonghak and Kim Changbong, were "purged." The government issued an order to remove their names from school textbooks; and in typical Orwellian fashion we would in unison all blot out their names with black ink or carve them out with a penknife. They had become "unpeople."

Because group activities were more important than academics, we spent large periods of time in the Youth Corps performing various services. When Kim Il Sung ordered that women should not wear pants in the summer, the children would patrol the streets and carefully check the clothes of pedestrians. If women were indeed wearing pants, or if anyone had forgotten to wear their Kim Il Sung pins on their jackets, we children would demand their names, and they would be reported immediately to their supervisors at work.

We were told that to defeat the American imperialists, our country would need to buy weapons abroad, so we were sent out for hours each day gathering scrap iron, bottles, and other recyclable products that could be sold for foreign currency. We were assigned quotas to fulfill, and children who failed to do so were admonished publicly. Who could gather the most became a great source of competition among us.

We were also instructed to search about and to collect the skins of rabbits and dogs, as well as (to this day I don't recall why) maggots. Maggots were most commonly found in the dungheaps at the public outhouses, where the toilets did not flush, and again we competed intensely. As for the dung itself, we were also required to collect that! When great heaps had accumulated, it was eventually shipped to farmers for use as fertilizer, and each person would be graded according to the quantity and quality of the dung collected. Later on, when rationing tickets were issued, these grades with which we had been rewarded were taken into account.

And yet the most difficult thing of all was to collect flowers. These we were required to place in front of the many statues of Kim Il Sung around our neighborhood. Since there were no flower shops in North Korea, the only way we could fulfill our quotas was to bribe the local greenhouse custodian.

These were the sort of activities that filled our days. Even during school vacations to take a holiday with our families was unthinkable. Instead we were obliged to use the extra time for Youth Corps projects.

During this period a second brother was born, an adorable baby whom my parents named Bum Soo.

One of the most unusual and special aspects of my childhood was that I became a movie star. Unbeknownst to me, I had been noticed and chosen by a casting agent who had visited our school one day looking for a boy and a girl for an upcoming film. It was to be called *Young Soo and Young Ok, Who Found Their Socialist Homeland*. Needless to say, it was a strange title by Western standards, but I was thrilled to be chosen for the part of Young Ok.

It was a propaganda film in every way, thinly disguised as drama. The story was of a family who became separated because of the division of North and South Korea. In the end the mother of the family gets taken away by American soldiers and separated from her family as punishment for giving shelter to

North Korean soldiers. Again I am reminded of Orwell, whom I have now read, when I think of such movies—they remind me, in retrospect, of the ritual in *1984* called the Two Minutes of Hate. The movies would end with the audience booing the Americans soundly and even throwing things at the screen.

I was still too young to understand any of this, however, and I was more occupied with the hero's welcome I received when I returned to school. When the movie was released, I actually became quite famous. People would recognize me as I walked down the streets and call me by my character's name, Young Ok. My mother would show me off to guests, as would the teachers at school. Only my father disapproved, and frowned every time the movie was mentioned.

I acted in one other film, a story about a young girl who is rescued by the People's Army from a fire as the soldiers retreated into the North during the Korean War. I played a supporting role as the lead character's best friend. As payment I received a new book bag and ten notebooks—hardly celebrity wages.

I received other offers in later years, but my father refused to let me act again. Instead I concentrated on my Youth Corps activities. Every morning at seven o'clock Pyongyang's only radio station would broadcast the Youth Corps song, which went as follows:

> *We are the young heroes of the Republic,*
> *Growing up as the Vanguard of Communism.*
> *Friends in the Youth Corps, raise the flag high!*
> *As sons and daughters of our President,*
> *Let us march onward with vigor!*

I was recruited as a Youth Corps leader and devoted most of my time to trying to mold my group into a model for the others. Though we were somewhat successful, I was not a good disciplinarian and could never, of my own volition, speak harshly of my friends.

When it came to grades, our results would be displayed publicly. There were four subjects in schools: revolution, academics, labor, and ethics. During the hour for discussing revolution, for example, the teacher would hold aloft a photo from

19

Kim Il Sung's past and ask a student to explain it. The child would come forward, both hands raised, eyes fixed on the photograph, and explain with reverence, "This photo shows the Great President giving directions for the proliferation of the armed struggle throughout the world. The Great President was at the time holding a conference of the Chosen People's Revolutionary Army at Karoon in 1930."

If the answer was spoken correctly, a red mark would be placed in the student's "Revolution" column on the bulletin board.

Because I was a Youth Corps leader, I was often called upon by the teacher to help discipline those students who did not perform as required. I remember when one student was castigated for failing to meet his quotas, each member of the class was asked to recite some criticism to his face. I trembled when it became my turn, for I hated having to impugn one of my fellow students; but the teacher's steely gaze was fixed on me, and I said as resolutely as possible, "You claim to have not met your quotas because you didn't have time. And yet yesterday I myself saw you playing with other children. I find it hard to believe that you have time to play but not to work. Such an excuse shows you have violated the lesson of Our Great Leader, who teaches us to be faithful to a group life."

I was applauded, and the teacher nodded her approval. But I did not feel happy as I sat down and listened woodenly to the next student, a girl named Sun Young, who was always happy to denounce someone. "Comrade student, you don't deserve to study in the bosom of Father President. You should be expelled from school at once."

These sessions took place two or three times a week. Eventually we came to look for things to criticize in our own families. To criticize nothing at all was made to seem the worst thing we could do.

During my last year in high school I was accepted by the Biology Department of Kim Il Sung University. This is the only North Korean university in any way comparable to its American counterparts, and only the children of high-ranking government officials could attend. As in all other schooling in

North Korea, the curriculum emphasized ideological studies, and most of the time was spent learning about the philosophy of Kim Il Sung.

Prior to matriculation I spent six months in military training, which was required of all students. Once school started, I was amused to note that the university was organized along military lines. A class was called a platoon, a department a company, the undergraduate group a battalion, and so on. The class leader was called lieutenant, and the Student Department head was captain.

Graduates of Kim Il Sung University were all but guaranteed good jobs for the rest of their lives, and only the most privileged could attend. But privileged though I was, I had trouble keeping up with my studies, because most of my spare time was spent doing mandatory farm work in the nearby countryside. My father then suggested that I transfer to Pyongyang Foreign Language College, which also seemed to guarantee a good job after graduation, particularly for a woman. My father arranged for me to take the entrance exam, which I passed, and I enrolled as a major in Japanese language.

It was a fateful decision. Had I not transferred to Pyongyang and studied Japanese, I would never have been recruited as an agent. At the time, of course, I had no idea what consequences this change would bring. . . .

As required, I also continued my military training. We would be taken to boot camps in the countryside, spending long days learning to shoot rifles and march in columns. It was especially difficult for women, who under the Communist regime were considered to be the equals of men and were required to undergo the same rigorous training. Unfortunately, however, the camps were in no way equipped for females. We were forced to change in cramped closets, and often ran out of menstrual pads.

It was a grueling life. We spent days on end marching up mountains. We learned to identify and use various types of weapons and motorized military vehicles. We were poorly fed, and many of us lost a lot of weight. Often, during the longer marches, I had trouble keeping up. The lieutenant in charge, a handsome man in his mid-twenties, would drop back and urge me along. "Come on, Hyun Hee, no hanging back. Being a woman is no excuse. Men and women will be treated equally here."

I noticed, however, that women often seemed to be considered liabilities, not assets. As a result we were drilled more strictly and more frequently. I resented the double standard, but in the end I felt equal in prowess to any man.

By the end of our service we were marching twenty miles at a stretch while carrying thirty-pound packs. We were adept at firing machine guns, pistols, and could even drive tanks. We threw hand grenades, operated the antiaircraft guns in mock air raids, and learned to fire antitank missiles.

I felt enormous relief returning to college in Pyongyang and worked hard trying to catch up in my studies. Men and women were not allowed to date, but a few brave souls would sometimes take the risk. Those caught were expelled, and some were even deported to labor camps in the far North. Physical exams were required at regular intervals, which for women included a gynecological checkup. This way the authorities could be sure we were still virgins.

Looking back, I wonder how I found time to sleep. On weekends we would be off working in coal mines, helping out, and there were always revolutionary rallies to attend. It seems a miracle that I learned any Japanese at all, but in fact I began to be fluent and earned top marks.

During my second year in college, when I was eighteen, I was called to the dean's office one day. There I met a man with a flag-shaped badge on his chest, which indicated that he was from the Central Party.

"Comrade Hyun Hee," he said as I walked into the room. "I trust you have studied the many virtues of Our Dear Leader, Kim Jung Il. Why not recite the first one that comes to mind?"

I hesitated for a moment in confusion and then quickly recalled the Mount Paektu incident where Kim Jung Il had visited the battlefield where his father, Kim Il Sung, had won a great victory and ordered the workers to be more enthusiastic about restoring the site and gave them some useful instructions to help them along.

When I finished reciting, he asked me, "Where does your father work and what is his rank?"

I told him.

"Excellent. One more thing: Are you doing well in school?"

He knew this already, because I was a member of the Historical Research Center for Kim Il Sung, which consisted of the top ten female students in the college. "Of course," I replied somewhat indignantly.

I was dismissed. Later that week the female students were required to line up in the gymnasium so that a group of visiting men could look us over. They took some notes as they appraised us, and whenever they came upon a pretty girl, they would ask her name.

As we were leaving the gymnasium, I was taken aside by one of the men and told to report to the Section 1 Building of the Party the following week.

I had no choice but to show up as ordered, and a group of officers were waiting to question me. I felt awkward and uncomfortable, but I gave a polite bow, and the interview began.

"What are the four basic principles of the Party?" one asked.

"Deification, Creed, Absoluteness, and Unconditional Acceptance," I replied automatically.

"Why do you study Japanese?"

"I am learning Japanese to help our nation prevail over Japan so that Korea can be reunified."

"What will you do after school?"

"I will do whatever the Party tells me to."

"Very good. Now recite from memory the first chapter of *The Memory of Kim Jung Sook, Kim Jung Il's Wife*."

I was able to recite the lines almost without hesitation. He seemed amazed by my memory.

"How are your grades?"

"They are outstanding, sir."

He handed me an excerpt from *Kim Il Sung's Memoirs* in Japanese and asked me to translate it on the spot. I did so without error.

"Excellent, excellent." He paused for a moment, and then his tone grew serious. "Kim Hyun Hee, would you be willing to die for the Party? For you realize that an appointment to the

23

Party could bring you not only the highest honors but death as well?"

I could hardly breathe, I was so taken aback by the question, but I was determined not to show it. "Of course," I replied firmly. "I will do everything the Party asks me to, even if it means giving my life."

He made a note on the pad in front of him. "Do you have a boyfriend?"

"No sir."

"Good. Now you shall be given a physical exam." I was led to a doctor's office and examined and then made to wait in the anteroom for a while. Soon I was called in again.

The leader of the interview, who was named Special Agent Chung, stood as I walked in, holding out his hand. "Congratulations, Comrade Kim Hyun Hee. You have been chosen by the Party."

I knew that I should have felt happy, but I was bewildered and apprehensive. Everything had happened so quickly. Still, I took his hand. I tried to smile and appear grateful, but I honestly didn't know what to make of all this.

"You've been requested to pack immediately," he continued. "You can spend the night with your family, and tomorrow you'll leave."

He accompanied me back to the college, where I had only a moment to say good-bye to my professors. They seemed proud to learn of my good fortune and wished me well. Within an hour I was home, accompanied by Special Agent Chung, and giving my mother the astonishing news.

When I told her about the appointment, I could see immediately that she was shocked, though she did her best not to show it. She politely offered Special Agent Chung dinner, but he declined. He said that I would be picked up the following day, and left.

My sister and brothers, when they learned the news, were ecstatic. My mother remained silent, however, as she prepared our dinner. At length she asked, not looking up, "Does this mean you will be gone for good?"

I hesitated before answering. "I don't know, Mother."

She continued to chop vegetables and then dropped them

into the stir-fry. "I hope your father takes this well," she remarked, and would say no more.

As it turned out, my father did not come home for several hours. I spent the evening packing, and as I did, I came across some embroidery my mother had made when she was in high school. She had given me the design when I had entered college, and it had great sentimental value to me.

I decided to give the embroidery to Hyun Ok. When I handed it to her, I felt as though I was passing her my position as first daughter of the family and leaving forever. "Take good care of it," I said. "And if I ever return, I want it back!"

At that instant we both burst into tears and remained in a fierce embrace until our mother called us for dinner.

It was midnight before my father came home and learned what had happened. He was stupefied and kept asking me the same questions over and over, as if he couldn't understand my answers. For a long while he was silent and then said with resignation, "Sit down and listen, Hyun Hee. I've always hoped that you would become an ordinary housewife and be a good mother to your children. But it is also a worthy honor to dedicate one's life to one's country. Please remember this at all times: You can survive even if you are thrown into a tiger's den if you can maintain your concentration. Do your best. I'm very proud of you."

My mother began to cry, and I felt guilty when I returned to my room. I sat for some time with my brothers and sister, looking at family photographs and remembering our old days together. Though I was sad to leave, I knew it was a great honor to be chosen by the Party. I told myself that every child has to leave home at some point and that I could hardly ask for anything better.

The next morning I was up early. No one spoke much during breakfast, and I could see that my mother's eyes were swollen from grief.

At ten o'clock Special Agent Chung arrived. He exchanged greetings with my father and added, "Don't worry about Hyun Hee. The Party will provide everything for her. We'll even find her a husband. Leave everything to us."

"Thank you," my father replied gravely. "She has brought

glory to our family, and we will not worry. I shall be eternally grateful to the Party."

How can I forget the day I left my family? My father kept looking at me with sad eyes. My mother and my sister were crying; only my brothers were acting cheerful, though I could tell it was strained.

"Good-bye," they chorused, one after the other, like an echo.

I can still hear those voices to this day. I can still hear that echo.

CHAPTER TWO

I FELT A surge of pride as the car sped through the suburbs of Pyongyang. Whenever we passed children, they would salute the car in scout style. As we reached a checkpoint on the outskirts of the city, the car was waved through without stopping.

As we headed along the road toward Pyongsung City, the car suddenly slowed and turned onto an unpaved mountain road. Sometime later we passed a security checkpoint, where the guard on duty gave us a sharp salute. Beyond the checkpoint was an industrial farm, a huge expanse of sheds and buildings where quails were raised. We continued past the farm, and the road became quite isolated.

"Have you ever been to a place like this?" asked Chung. "At night tigers come down from the mountains."

I didn't like the fact that he was trying to frighten me. I gave him an angry look.

But he didn't even notice and just continued. "From now on you must never use or reveal your real name. You are now Kim Ok Hwa, and don't forget it. Under no circumstances are you to mention your birth name, especially to any new friends you may meet."

Not long after this the car stopped at one of a series of buildings, and we were met by a tall woman, who looked about fifty
years of age. She welcomed me and showed me to my room.
Next to it there was a bathroom with a tub and shower, and
fresh clothes had been provided for me. For a while I soaked
myself in the tub and wondered about my new surroundings.
Following my bath I went directly to bed, but all night I couldn't
sleep. I kept listening to the eerie sound of the wind in the
trees, feeling the extreme loneliness of this place. I was frightened now that I was on my own, and the thought of wandering
tigers outside did not ease my fears. It was dawn before I finally
fell asleep.

When I awoke the next morning, I was served the finest
breakfast since I'd left Cuba—fried eggs, toast, milk, butter,
and potatoes. The bread was of a fine, light texture, a quality
impossible to find in Pyongyang, and I felt somewhat ashamed
to be eating so well.

After breakfast I was introduced to my new roommate, who
I was told would be my partner throughout my training. Her
name was Kim Sook Hee, a pretty young woman with large,
shining eyes and a ready smile. She was a year younger than I.
Over the next few years she would become like a sister to me,
one of the dearest friends I ever had.

Special Agent Chung walked into the room and sat down.
"Good morning," he said, smiling at us. "Now that you're both
here, we can go over some of the rules. You're never to leave
the installation during the day, and at night you are permitted
only a brief walk. You must inform the cook before you go, and
take care to avoid any outsiders who may be present—the de-
livery men, the chauffeurs, and so on. When you go out, you
should wear sunglasses and a mask, which we'll provide for
you, and carry an umbrella to hide your faces should you happen to encounter anyone.

"You are to finish breakfast each morning by eight o'clock.
Before leaving for classes you should take half an hour to read
and reread *Selected Writings of Kim Il Sung* and *History of the
Revolutionary Struggle*. Is all this clear?"

We assured him that it was.

Later that day we were visited by a man introduced to us as
Deputy Minister Kang. He was of medium height, with a round

face and small, venomous eyes. We sat with him in the library, and he spoke to us bluntly and without pleasantries.

"As you know, the Party's goal is the unification of Korea within this generation. Keeping that in mind, we have high hopes that you two will become excellent warriors. Since you were chosen from among many candidates, I trust that you won't disappoint us."

He paused to let his ominous words sink in and then continued. "In a few days' time you will be transferred to a school where many of the great special agents have received their training."

"We will not fail," we responded in unison, as if on cue.

"Do you know why we use women in espionage warfare?" he continued. "Because of their beauty. If it becomes necessary, you will be expected to sell your bodies. Moreover, if you need to remain in a foreign country legally, you'll have to marry someone we choose for you. I trust that you understand this."

We said nothing, but I know we were scared, and frankly sick to our stomachs. And later that evening, as we lay in bed, I said, "Sook Hee, do you think you could go through with it? To give yourself to a stranger, I mean?"

She sighed. "I really don't know. And you?"

"Me neither."

When next she spoke, there was bitterness in her tone. "I suppose it's not for us to choose, is it?"

I felt as bitter as she sounded.

CHAPTER THREE

LATER IN THE WEEK we were transferred to Keumsung Military College and began our training in earnest. Even my rigorous stint in the army could not have forewarned me of what we encountered here.

Keumsung was in a forbidding valley beneath Mount Ipbul, miles from any civilization except a few small villages, which were scattered throughout the region. The complex sprawled across a good deal of territory, because there were thousands of students being trained there. Intelligence agents were trained in a secret valley apart from the main body of the college.

We were put in a small house with a kitchen, laundry room, and library. We were given a tight schedule from which we were never permitted to deviate:

0600–0700	Wake up, clean house, wash clothes
0700–0730	Breakfast
0730–0830	Morning reading of Kim Il Sung's philosophy and virtues
0830–1300	Morning classes
1300–1600	Lunch and rest

1600–1730	Afternoon classes
1730–1900	Exercise
1900–2000	Dinner
2000–2100	Martial arts
2100–2200	Night march
2200–2300	Study
2300	Bedtime

We were pushed to exhaustion, to the limits of what our minds and bodies could endure. We practiced our shooting skills with every variety of gun. We lived for days in the open, sleeping in foxholes. On Kim Il Sung's birthday we marched one hundred miles over three days—this was known as the March of Loyalty. We learned how to drive cars at high speeds and to develop film with improvised darkrooms. And all the while we read dozens of volumes of writings by Kim Il Sung.

We trained in the martial arts. Women were expected to be able to defeat two or three grown men at once, and I developed a self-confidence I'd never had before. We also trained in knife combat, using 25-centimeter plastic knives (about 10 inches).

Our firearms training was not confined to shooting. We were required to take each gun apart and reassemble it, and fix it if it was out of order. Our targets were tiny bull's-eyes 100 yards away, and I hit mine 90 percent of the time.

We were shown espionage films twice a week, which were full of propaganda about the decadence of Western society and detailed the exploits of famous agents of years past.

Sundays were our only free days, and we were usually so exhausted that we didn't get out of bed.

My Japanese-language teacher was named Eun Hae, and we developed a close friendship. Through the cook I learned a bit of her history, which was tragic. She was from Tokyo and had married after graduating from high school. She had given birth to a boy and a girl and then divorced her husband a short time later. One day, when playing with her children at the beach, she was abducted by North Korean agents and transported to the camp. During her imprisonment she became severely ill and nearly died. When at last she recovered, she refused to eat and spoke only of missing her children. But the North Koreans waited her out, hinting that she might be released in the indefinite future if she followed their orders. Eventually she had no choice but to adjust to her new life.

Though I sympathized with her situation, I thought the sacrifice of one Japanese woman to the cause of Korean unification was justified, especially considering that Japan had occupied and raped Korea for forty years. Now, looking back, I am ashamed of myself. This incident is a prime example of the unconscionable barbarity of the North Korean government and its agents.

Because Eun Hae was so miserable, she would frequently get drunk and could occasionally be unpleasant. But despite all this, she was an excellent teacher and I found myself liking her more and more. She would often speak of her children and of Tokyo, each time hoping that she would soon be returned to Japan. I don't know if she ever was.

We became friends and confidantes, and she looked forward to our time together. Her assignment was nothing less than to transform me into a Japanese woman, so that once I was in the field, it would be impossible to discern that I was really North Korean.

There was a village a mile or two away from our house, and we were of course required to stay away from it. But Eun Hae insisted, one Sunday evening, that we visit the village, because she had never seen ordinary North Koreans before. We found a decrepit cluster of houses and filthy children running around the streets, some naked. I was ashamed at this and tried to pull Eun Hae away. But she stared at the children with tears in her eyes. They were bringing out her maternal instincts.

"So this is your brave new world, Ok Hwa," she said with unmitigated scorn. "I pity you."

Another good friend at the camp was the cook, a woman in her mid-forties named Wul Chi, who also had a tragic history. She had fallen in love in her teens with a lathe operator, but had been forced by her mother to marry a coal miner. Living in near-poverty in the backwoods village of Samjiuon, Wul Chi spent several miserable years while her husband had numerous affairs with other women.

One day her husband was struck and killed by a mine cart.

At his funeral she met the lathe operator with whom she'd first been in love. But he now had a family of his own, and though he still loved her, there was nothing he could do.

Wul Chi eventually found work teaching cooking classes at a college before her recruitment to the training camp. She loved the solitude of Keumsung, because, as she joked, there were fewer people to bother her. She doubled as our "house-mother," and we had to report to her whenever we wanted to take a walk or leave the general vicinity. But she was a generous person and frequently permitted us to do as we pleased.

During the years that followed, I was occasionally permitted to visit my family, but these were sad occasions. My parents were always reluctant to see me leave, and I, at the time, some-how felt ashamed of their attachment to me, which is what any fully indoctrinated North Korean would be expected to feel. It was not part of one's patriotic duty to become overly attached to one's relatives, and at the time my main concern was with my newfound status as an agent trainee. During this period my youngest brother, Bum Soo, became ill with skin cancer, which doctors told us would ultimately be terminal.

My mother was openly and vocally unhappy about my being gone, but I knew my father missed me just as much. Through-out my childhood he had been touchingly devoted to me, al-ways calling me his Little Princess. In many ways my father was an enigmatic man. I knew that he was proud of me and that as a Party official he was among the most privileged of North Koreans, but something told me that he resented the government dearly for taking me away.

Love, unfortunately, was not part of Kim Jung Il's national agenda.

CHAPTER FOUR

WHEN I HAD been at the camp for three years, I was required to take what was known as the Final Exam, which was designed to assess what I had learned thus far. It was by far the most grueling and nerve-racking period of my training, because students who failed the exam twice would be expelled from the Party and disgraced for the rest of their lives.

An entire week was set aside for the exam, which was divided into three major parts—physical, written, and field test. Each part was rigorously evaluated and scored on a basis of one hundred possible points. To pass the exam, students were required to achieve ninety points in each of the three parts.

For weeks before the exam I felt a constant sense of anxiety, as did the other students who would be participating. All that we had knocked ourselves out working for during the past three years was being put to the test. We had been told that only a third of all participants regularly passed the exam. In this fashion the Party was able to retain only the best people as its operatives.

The first day of the exam dawned cool and gray. It was September, and already there was rime on the ground, which portended the impending winter. I rose at six A.M., as required, my stomach in knots. I dressed in an athletic uniform and tried to eat breakfast, but I was so nervous that my hands were shaking, and I literally had trouble bringing the food to my mouth. Moreover my throat was constricted with tension, and I could swallow only with difficulty.

Sook Hee was taking the test with me, and she was just as anxious as I was. We spoke little during breakfast, each of us trying to dispel our fears in some way or another. I recalled some lessons I had been given in Transcendental Meditation and tried to repeat the *Om* mantra to myself. But within moments my mind wandered, and I would find myself shivering nervously and feeling no better than before.

At six-thirty we heard a whistle outside, which was the signal to begin, and we trooped outside into the courtyard. There were about fifteen of us all told, of whom a third were women. Off to one side stood two instructors, one male and one female, who were dressed in combat fatigues and wore green military caps. When we had all assembled, the male instructor, a tall, muscular man named Rae Hong, clapped his hands for our attention.

"Comrades!" he shouted, his breath emerging in vaporous clouds in the chilly air. "We are now ready to begin the first part of the exam. This will consist of a fifteen-kilometer [roughly ten miles] run around the camp, using a series of mountain trails along the eastern valley. The route has been marked with orange flags, and both myself and Comrade Myung"—he gestured to the female instructor—"will accompany you as monitors. Other instructors will be waiting at the finish line, on the other side of the camp, where they will record your times. The faster you complete the course, the higher your score. Anyone who does not complete the course will receive no points, thereby disqualifying himself for the entire exam. Is this clear?"

"Yes, sir!" we chorused.

"Get ready," he shouted, turning toward the road. When we were all ready, he blew his whistle and jogged off down the road, and we quickly rushed after him.

His pace was too quick for me. Rather than worry about keeping up with him, I set my own pace and concentrated on establishing a good rhythm. As in any race, some of the others were rushing forward at speeds that would be impossible to maintain for very long. I tried to ignore them and concentrate on my own performance. At all costs I must not stop, and I thought to myself that only a full collapse would stop me.

The first kilometer was pure agony. My thoughts were wandering all over the place, urging me to forget the whole race and sit down and rest. I thrust them aside and tried to think of anything else—a conversation the previous night with Sook Hee, something I'd read recently. In this fashion I was able to complete the first kilometer, and after that point I had settled into an easy stride.

Our course wandered up into the mountains, which added to the grueling trek. The valley below us was beautiful in the early autumn, and already splashes of color were appearing in places. The mountains around us were peaceful and still, and there was a distant chorus of birdsong. The temperature gradually warmed, and soon I was sweating profusely.

As the race progressed, we began to straggle from our original group. Some of the runners dropped behind, while others were far ahead. Sook Hee and I pretty much stayed together through the whole thing, occasionally muttering words of encouragement to each other.

After two thirds of the race had been run, the trail began to descend from the mountains, and this made it much easier to keep my pace. But by now, ten kilometers into the race, my legs were beginning to ache. Even this, however, was not my main concern. I was bent at all costs upon maintaining my rate of breathing, with one breath for every four strides. I knew that once I lost this rhythm, I would almost surely not finish.

As the race neared its end, we came upon a few casualties. One man and one woman had collapsed at various points along the trail and were sobbing helplessly in the grass. I felt a pang of sympathy for them as I passed, but there was nothing I could do. I prayed silently that they would pass the next time.

During the final two kilometers my lungs began to burn, and I was forced to take a breath first at every three strides, and then at every two. Sook Hee was stumbling beside me, a look of grim determination on her face, her eyes fixed forward in anticipation of the finish line. She was breathing in ragged gasps, and at one point I yelled at her, "Come on, Sook Hee! Not much farther! We're almost there!" She responded by rolling her eyes, but I knew that my encouragement had worked.

None of us knew precisely where the finish line would be, which only added to the mental agony of the race; there was no fixed point to aim for. But at long last, just as I felt I could go no farther, I saw a group of runners who'd already finished the race standing around and talking to Instructor Rae Hong. Other instructors were waiting with stopwatches. I pushed forward across the finish line and promptly collapsed, Sook Hee beside me.

"Two hours, four minutes, and twenty-seven seconds for comrades Ok Hwa and Sook Hee!" shouted one of the time-keepers, making a note on her clipboard. "Well done, comrades! That's worth ninety-three and a half points!"

"Bloody hell." Sook Hee panted. "If it hadn't been for you, Ok Hwa, I never would have made it. I feel half dead."

"Me too," I replied, still struggling for breath. I rolled onto my back and gazed at the sky, which had cleared into a deep blue. My head was throbbing, and I felt dizzy. I thought for a moment I would pass out, and Rae Hong strode over and pulled me to my feet.

"You should walk around a bit," he said. "The worst thing you can do is lie down. It's bad for your heart. You'll feel all right soon."

I nodded and walked around the courtyard. About six runners had finished the race already—five men and one woman— and Sook Hee and I made it eight. Over the next half hour a few others straggled in, and only three had been forced to quit altogether. It was now barely nine A.M., and there would be plenty more to come that day.

Rae Hong told us to take showers and change uniforms before reporting to the Athletic Center at ten o'clock, when the exam would resume. I watched him walk off in amazement. We had just run fifteen kilometers, and he wasn't even breathing hard.

Sook Hee and I staggered into our house and stripped off our clothes. I let her use the shower and instead took a long hot bath for myself, which made me feel both refreshed and exhausted at the same time. I dressed into another training uniform and drank a tall glass of orange juice before walking over to the Athletic Center.

This was a long narrow building with two gymnasiums, a weight room, a swimming pool, and a large square room with mirrors and martial arts equipment. The instructors were in the weight room, and since it was still a few minutes before ten, I spent some time stretching with the other students while we waited for the test to resume.

"Right!" said Rae Hong at precisely ten o'clock. "Let's continue. We'll start in the weight room, where each one of you will be required to bench-press the maximum weight of which you are capable. You will then do as many pull-ups as you are able on the chinning bar. Comrade Ok Hwa, we'll start with you."

Nervously I stood and walked over to the bench press, where two muscle-bound attendants were waiting to assist me. I tried to recall the weight I usually trained at, which was 50 kilograms—roughly 100 pounds.

"I'll try seventy-five kilos," I said, sitting on the bench. The attendants loaded the barbell with the weights and placed it on the rack. I lay down under it. This was about 150 pounds, and quite a stretch for a woman of my stature. I had never lifted this kind of weight before—70 kilos was my best effort to date—and I was already fatigued from the run. Still, I would be given one more try if I failed, so I might as well aim high.

I did series of quick, deep breaths, sending as much oxygen as possible into my blood. I gripped the iron barbell and gathered my strength to lift it from the rack.

With a cry I pushed, and the weights rose ponderously into the air. The barbell teetered for a moment, and I fought to regain control. I then lowered the bar until it touched my chest, as required. Summoning every ounce of strength, I exhaled and pushed the barbell upward. About halfway up it stopped. I gave a shout, my face contorting, and pushing even harder. Miraculously I was able to fully extend my arms and complete the exercise. The attendants took the weight from my hands and replaced it on the rack.

There was a cheer from the onlookers. Somewhat dazed, I rose from the bench and sat down. "Excellent!" boomed Rae

Hong. "Score ninety-six points for Ok Hwa! Would you like to try again?"

"No, sir," I replied.

"Very well. Next!"

Sook Hee, when her turn came, was able to press 65 kilos, a very respectable figure worth 92 points. The best score came from a stocky, muscle-bound man named Kim Bong, who, in a fit of snarling ecstasy, pressed more than 200 kilos and earned 10 bonus points, for a total of 110, for his efforts.

Next we moved on to pull-ups. I had practiced these every day for the past three years, and I could generally complete about fifteen. That day I managed seventeen, and earned 94 points. Sook Hee completed sixteen, and once again Kim Bong was the high achiever with forty-six.

"Into the second gymnasium!" shouted Myung, when we were through in the weight room.

The next test was designed to rate our speed. The gym was perhaps 50 meters in length (about 54 yards), and each student was required to run from one wall to the other and then back again. We would be given three attempts.

I myself felt confident for this race. For a woman of my height I was fairly quick, and there was not an ounce of fat on me after three years of intensive training. My best time was 19.4 seconds, which was not bad considering that when we touched the opposite wall, we were forced to slow down before making the return run. Sook Hee did even better, finishing in 19.1 seconds. She received 95 points for this event, and I received 94.8.

It was noon by then, and we were allowed to break for lunch, most of us thoroughly exhausted. That day we received double rations of everything, and I was still hungry when I was finished. The next event did not begin until 13:00 hours, and Sook Hee and I took twenty minutes to collapse on our beds and try to regain our strength.

"I can't believe how hard they're pushing us," she said, massaging her legs.

"It's not over yet," I replied. "But all I can say is, we've come a long way since we turned eighteen and started army training. I could barely run a mile then."

"I could barely *walk* a mile then." She laughed.

At 1300 hours we were back in the Athletic Center, this time in the *dojung*, or martial arts room. We had been required to change into *ghis*—the white pajamalike uniforms used by martial artists.

Our martial arts training derived from a variety of styles, all of them Korean, including Tae Kwan Do, Tung Soo Do, and Hapkido. These similar but nevertheless distinct styles had been molded into a hybrid martial art, which was used to train the agents. Our belt system progressed as follows: White for beginners, and then Yellow, Green, Blue, Red, Brown, and then ten degrees of Black. There were few martial artists alive who had legitimately reached the upper Black Belt degrees, but our instructor, Kai Cheon, was Fifth-Degree in each of the three Korean arts. After three years of training we had all reached at least First Degree, but afterward it generally took years to attain each successive degree.

Kai had two assistants, both Third-Degree Black Belts, named Yung Lui and Kang Khil. After leading us through some warm-ups, he sat himself at the head of the room with Kang Khil beside him, holding a clipboard. Yung Lui stood nearby, and Rae Hong and Myung, themselves Second-Degree Black Belts, were seated nearby.

"We shall start with unarmed combat," said Rae Hong. "Each of you comrades will fight for five minutes with Yung Lui. In view of the accuracy required during this testing, you'll be fighting full-contact—no pads. The men will have groin protectors but nothing more. Most techniques will be legal—you can kick below the legs and to the head, and you can apply throws and locks, but we will be grading your restraint as well as your skill. A technique that is solidly delivered but controlled enough to do little harm will receive the highest grade. Any deliberately broken bones will result in that student's immediate disqualification. Understood? Good. Let's begin."

I was thankful that I didn't have to go first. I had never fought Yung Lui before and was glad for the chance to observe his style. He was a tall, wiry man with great hand and foot speed, capable of executing the most complicated kicks imaginable. I had once seen him break a cement tile that had been placed vertically eight feet off the ground. He had jumped up, spun around in midair, and brought his leg around in a perfect spinning heel kick to shatter the tile.

Some fighters are counterattackers, but Yung Lui fought more aggressively, initiating attacks of his own accord. He feinted beautifully, delivering a flurry of blows to the first student with such ease and dexterity that I quickly grew doubtful that I could do anything against him. At the end of five minutes the student, a young man, was battered and bloody, but still earned 90 points for holding his own against a master.

When three more students had gone, my own turn came. I rose, jogged out to the center of the floor, bowed to Yung Lui, and then we both bowed to the instructors. Kai nodded and signaled for us to begin.

Yung Lui came for me right away. The fact that I was female meant nothing in this environment, and I had seen women receive broken noses and cracked ribs as often as the men. He launched a series of kicks at me, which I evaded with difficulty. I had no illusions of counterattacking so soon. I was trying to stay on my feet.

At length he backed off and waited for me. As the lesser-ranking student I was now required to attack him quickly or risk being penalized for stalling. Left foot leading, I aimed a few quick punches at his face. He raised his arms to block, and simultaneously I hooked my left foot behind his ankle and executed a perfect sweep, pulling his leg from under him and sending him to the floor. His other leg came around immediately for a thrust kick into my stomach, and I was driven backward. He sprang to his feet and followed with a hard punch to my ribs and another to my chin. Frightened, angry, and desperate, I ignored the pain and grabbed his leading hand, yanking him closer for a roundhouse kick into the gut. He was momentarily staggered, and I grabbed his shoulders, stepped behind him, and threw him to the floor. As expected, he lashed out with his foot, but I was ready this time. I caught his leg in midair and directed a kick of my own into his groin.

"Break!" called Kai. "Score an early round for Ok Hwa!"

Yung Lui got to his feet. He was angry now, and his next attacks were sharper and faster. He delivered several glancing blows to my midsection that I could not block, and in a moment he would have me. I managed to duck under his guard and deliver an elbow into his sternum before grabbing his leg and throwing him to the floor. He responded expertly, bringing his other leg around until he'd locked my own legs in a scissors-hold and pulled me down in turn. With his legs tightly enclosing mine, he was already sitting up and aiming a chop for my face. I caught his wrist and bent the hand back into a lock, and reflexively his scissors-hold loosened.

"Break!" called Rae Hong.

We both stood, bowed to Kai, and then to each other. There was a pause as the instructors computed their scores and averaged them together. I took my seat and waited.

"For Comrade Ok Hwa . . . ninety-eight!"

There was a brief round of applause. I was stunned. I had managed to hold my own against an accomplished fighter, though I knew that in real combat he would be more than a match for me. Still, I had gotten the better of Yung Lui this time, and I lowered my eyes, not daring to look at him.

As if stung by his poor showing against me, Yung Lui proceeded to batter every other student around the floor unmercifully, trapping them in painful locks, flipping them through the air, catching them with beautifully executed kicks. When all the students had finished, Yung Lui sat down, and Kang Khil stood.

"Now we begin the second event," said Kai. "Each student will face Comrade Kang Khil, who will be wielding a twenty-five-centimeter plastic knife. You will be given three attempts to disarm him and then use the knife yourself or overcome him some other way. Questions? No? Let's begin!"

I was the third student to face Kang Khil. After the bows we circled each other warily. The plastic blade of the knife was designed to retract into the handle, as a measure of how far a real knife would have penetrated. Kang Khil feinted at me, his black eyes locked into mine. The gaze can be a powerful weapon among good martial artists, and I forced myself to concentrate on his knife hand. Suddenly he sprang forward, cat-quick, the knife angling for my stomach. I was so surprised that I couldn't even block his arm. He pressed the knife into my abdomen and the blade retreated fully into the handle.

"First round to Kang Khil!" shouted Kai. "Come on, Ok Hwa! Concentrate!"

Chagrined, I assumed a combat stance and circled with Kang Khil again. This time I did watch his eyes, trusting that they would betray his intentions. He switched the knife from hand to hand, smirking slightly, biding his time. On impulse I pivoted on the ball of my foot and launched a spinning back kick at his face. To my surprise the blow landed. Kang Khil stepped back with a cry, one hand reaching up for his face. I followed with two hard punches to his sternum and could have finished him off right then had I acted sensibly. But instead of driving my knee into his groin or aiming a controlled chop at his throat, which would have caused the judges to suspend the round, I grabbed his knife hand and jammed my other arm behind his elbow. The pressure caused him to release the knife, which I scooped up instantly. But Kang Khil had recovered from my attack and launched a front kick at my chest as I bent over. I took the full force of the blow and was driven back ten feet before falling ignominiously on my rear end. He was after me right away, but at least I had retained my grip on the knife. I climbed heavily to my feet and stabbed at him. He stopped in his tracks, avoiding the thrust, and then assumed a combat stance. We circled each other again, but now I had the advantage.

He advanced on me, forcing me back, and he kept his front foot poised to kick. Kang Khil was a formidable opponent, built like a rock, and I had my doubts about whether I could get inside his guard. I decided to try a different ploy. I tossed the knife at him, and for a moment his eyes darted upward. In that brief time I drove the instep of my foot into his groin and then followed with a solid punch to the chin. Kang Khil, looking startled, fell back onto his own rear end!

"Break!" yelled Kai. "Ok Hwa has won!"

I helped a dazed Kang Khil to his feet. After bowing I sat down to await the score.

"Ninety-four!" shouted Rae Hong.

By then it was late afternoon, and there were no more events that day. Sook Hee and I returned to our house and were asleep by 1900 hours. I had surprised myself. I just might be special-agent material after all.

The next day was not nearly as strenuous as the first, consisting mostly of weapons testing.

In the first event we used high-powered rifles to hit bull's-eyes at a hundred meters' distance (about 109 yards). We were given fifty shots, and I hit the target forty-seven times. Sook Hee actually scored a perfect 50, as did many of the other students, and all of us scored well.

We were then tested in pistol shooting, only this time the target was only twenty-five meters away. I hit the target forty-six times again, a score surpassed only by Sook Hee, who again scored a perfect 50.

"I think you've found your niche," I said to her during lunch.

"I'm glad I'm doing something right," she replied. "After getting knocked around by Yung Lui yesterday I wasn't feeling very good about myself. And, boy, do my legs ache!"

"Mine too," I said, grinning. In fact I had barely been able to get out of bed this morning, I was so sore. Not to mention the various bruises sustained during the martial arts events the previous day.

The rest of the day continued in a similar vein, with events such as archery, knife throwing, and grenade lobbing. I did reasonably well in all events except the archery, where I scored only an 82. But my overall average for the physical section was well above 90, so I was not worried.

Our driving skills were also tested. We were required to navigate a Mercedes at high speeds through an obstacle course, which included poles, sheets of ice, and hairpin turns. Each of us was given two opportunities, and we were carefully timed. I always got a thrill from driving cars because they were so absent from everyday life in North Korea. People in Western countries drive them everywhere, but for me they were still a novelty. But my three years of performance-driving training had served me well, and I scored a 96, second-best in the class.

The physical section of the challenge was over, and my overall average was 94.63. Only two students had scored better, and only eleven of the original fifteen proceeded to the writing section.

In many respects the written test was even more difficult than the physical. The test was conducted in two four-hour sections on each of two days, and the subjects were extremely varied.

The whole first day was spent covering the philosophy and history of Kim Il Sung. There were no multiple-choice questions. There were two hundred purely factual questions that could be answered in a word or a sentence and then three essays that focused on North Korean socialist ideology. The latter were especially effective in determining how well we had digested our propaganda, with questions such as "In no more than ten pages briefly explain some of the many ways that the North Korean government is superior to capitalism."

During the second day we were tested on many different subjects—math, foreign languages, and so on. There was a whole section on weapons capabilities, with questions such as "What is the favored handgun of the KGB and how many rounds does it hold?" and "Name every plane used by the North Korean Army and its specifications."

I was nervous throughout the exam, and there were many questions that I could not answer. Moreover I had no idea what constituted the minimum required score of 90, since it was impossible to determine how the instructors were weighing each part of the exam. After the second day of the written section—and the fourth overall—I was physically and mentally drained. We had been excused all other duties during the week of the final exam, and I found myself sleeping ten hours a night. Sook Hee was faring no better.

Because there were only eleven students now, the tests were graded quickly. Three students were disqualified, and of the remaining eight I received the second-highest average—93. Sook Hee received a 92.18. We both crossed our fingers. Two down, one to go.

The last part of the final exam was perhaps the most difficult of all. For this section it was said that each student's test was individualized according to the intended function that person was to serve in the Intelligence agency. All tests were given individually, and in many different locations. It was called the field test because it was intended to simulate, as accurately as possible, a scenario that we might encounter as agents in the field.

My own field test was to take place that Friday evening, and I was briefed during the morning by Rae Hong as to what would be required.

"Your mission will commence just before sundown," he began. "About six miles north of this camp, just over Keumsung Mountain and through a pine forest, the Party has built a two-story mansion that is designed to approximate a foreign embassy, which we therefore nicknamed the Embassy. You'll be given a map of the grounds as well as a floor plan to the building. The building is surrounded by a wall, and the grounds are patrolled by guards. When you've looked at the floor plan, you'll note that there's a room containing a safe. Inside that safe are some documents in Japanese. Your job will be to infiltrate the embassy, memorize the documents, and return—without being captured—by oh six hundred hours tomorrow.

"Almost everything will be perfectly simulated. The embassy bedrooms will be occupied by agents impersonating diplomatic personnel. The guards will not know when you are coming. The agents who are impersonating the roles of guards and embassy personnel will grade your performance. Everything will be as authentic as possible—you'll have to watch for trip-wire alarms, hidden surveillance monitors, microphones—everything.

"For this test you will be supplied with the following: two pistols, an AK-forty-seven automatic rifle, three knives, a can of foam spray, a rope with grappling hooks, a flashlight, a stethoscope, glass cutters, a compass, and a lockpick. The knives will be plastic, and the guns will fire paint pellets, which will sting but not permanently injure. The guards in turn will have similar weapons. If you are shot, you will be well marked, and if you're shot in vital areas, your score will be reduced accordingly. The guns will be equipped with silencers, and you'll get eight clips total for the pistols and two for the automatic rifle. Since this is a test of our guardsmen as well, it will be considered permissible if you are forced to knock them unconscious unless they surrender first. We want this to be as realistic as possible.

"Once you recover the documents, you will be required to read and memorize them before replacing them. When you finally return, you will be interrogated as to the contents of those documents. Any questions?"

In truth I had plenty, but I could only stare at him with a stupefied expression on my face. I couldn't believe that I was being sent upon such an assignment. The thoroughness of my instructors astounded me. At length I found my voice.

"I assume, sir, that other students have taken this same test?"

"Of course," he replied, "or at least something very much like it. As an agent in the field you must be fully prepared for any eventuality, and only through these sorts of tests can we determine who is truly qualified to join Foreign Intelligence. That's why we go through the expense of maintaining this otherwise useless building."

"And what"—I tried to phrase the question as innocuously as possible—"what do I need to do to pass the test? Everything?"

He chuckled. "I can't tell you that. It's best if you concentrate on fulfilling the entire assignment. There are no such things as 'minimum requirements' in the field, Ok Hwa. You either accomplish your mission or you don't."

I nodded to show my understanding. I did not want to appear uneasy before him, but inside, my stomach was churning at the prospect of this "test." I wondered where I would possibly find the confidence to carry it off successfully. But what was the alternative? To refuse and thus be expelled from the Party altogether? No, I would have to grit my teeth and strengthen my resolve. I would simply do the best I could.

Rae Hong stood. "Well, if you've no further questions, I'll leave you alone for the afternoon. I'll have everything you need sent here within a few hours—the equipment, the clothes, everything. I'll be back around eighteen hundred hours to officially see you off. In the meantime, I suggest you rest. Oh, and don't speak of this to anybody. Understood?"

I nodded again, and Rae Hong let himself out. I returned to

my bedroom and threw myself on the bed. Sleep was out of the question. I was so nervous that I was shaking all over, my teeth chattering. I wrapped myself in the blankets and huddled miserably for several hours, dreading every passing moment. If I had felt confident about myself the past few days, I no longer felt so. My entire future in the Party hinged upon this one night, and I was terrified of failing.

Sook Hee was gone all afternoon, which probably helped. I don't think I could have kept my fears to myself, and I probably would have revealed everything to her. She was probably taking her own test at that very moment. I hoped that she was doing all right.

The afternoon advanced, and I managed a fitful nap before getting out of bed at 1730 hours. I walked into the living room, where a large trunk had been placed. Inside I found everything I would need—guns, clothes, accessories. Sighing, I brought the clothes back to my room and put them on.

I had been provided with a black jumpsuit, black shoes, and a black stocking mask that left only my eyes exposed, like some old Ninja. There was a shoulder holster for one pistol, a hip holster for the other. There was a belt where I could keep the knives, flashlight, and several clips of ammunition.

I also had a backpack for the rope, stethoscope, and the rest of the ammunition, not to mention a can of foam for the hidden cameras.

I was all suited up and ready at 1800 hours, when Rae Hong stopped by to see me off. He looked approvingly at my attire and said that he wished he had a camera.

I was in no mood for humor. The clothes were comfortable, but I felt frankly ridiculous with my mask and my AK-47 slung over my shoulder.

"Well, Comrade Ok Hwa," said Rae Hong, glancing at his watch. "You have twelve hours to fulfill your assignment. Good luck!"

"Thank you, sir," I mumbled through my mask, and stepped outside.

It was a clear, moonless evening, and the shadows were already lengthening. I set off in the direction of the compound at a good walk, moving along the trail over Keumsung Mountain and into the pinewood. I had memorized the route to the embassy, but I brought both maps just in case. I had determined the location of the safe—the library.

It was darker in the woods, and I had only my compass to guide me. I listened to the familiar sounds of the forest at dusk—the blackbirds finishing their chorus, the scurryings of smaller animals coming out to hunt. I also listened for the heavier footsteps of tigers. It was not impossible that I should encounter a tiger.

Soon it was fully dark. I walked as quietly as possible, half convinced that some of Rae Hong's operatives were lurking in the woods around me, marking my progress. I used the flashlight but covered the beam with my hand except when necessary. The forest settled into a nocturnal silence.

I continued in this fashion for what seemed like forever. The eerie silence of the forest, except for the occasional wind in the treetops, was disconcerting. I knew that part of this whole test would be psychological and that moving several miles through a forest at night alone would itself be a significant accomplishment. I often had the urge to run—but where to? There was no shelter nearby, and the only alternative I had was to turn back. I was not ready for that yet.

Suddenly I could see light in the distance through the trees. I snapped off my flashlight and tucked it in my belt. I put away the compass and crept quietly forward, from tree trunk to tree trunk. When I had covered perhaps ten yards, I found myself at the edge of the forest, looking at the front gates of the embassy compound.

Lamps had been set in the walls on either side of the gates, and a guard stood next to each lamp. There was also a small guardhouse, which was lit from within. The walls were of white stucco and perhaps fifteen feet high. Beyond the walls, if I remembered correctly from the map I'd been given, would be a series of flowerbeds and a long, sloping front lawn that led to the house itself, visible in the distance through the gates.

I observed the guards for a while. Besides the two on duty there seemed to be another inside the guardhouse, which doubtless had a phone line to the embassy. After a time a patrol passed, three strong, talking among themselves and waving to the sentries as they walked by.

Remaining within the shelter of the trees, I moved along the perimeter of the grounds to the right of the gates. When I reached the corner, I continued along the next wall, running toward the house itself. Another patrol passed, and I sank back into the shadows until they were out of sight. I then fixed the grappling hook to the end of the rope, stepped out of the woods, and threw the rope over the wall. The hook caught. I pulled myself upward until I was atop the wall, where I paused briefly to gather my rope before jumping down to the other side.

I found myself on the front lawn of the embassy, about a hundred feet from the house itself and two hundred from the gates. I sank to the ground. Lanterns had been placed at regular intervals along the gravel drive that led from the gates to the front doors, and other light was leaking outside from inside the building itself. I noted another patrol walking near the house, moving away from me. Staying close to the wall, I darted forward until I was level with the house itself.

The house was constructed in the neoclassical style, with Greek pillars and a wide terrace in front of the building. Perhaps fifty feet of open lawn lay between me and the house. Looking into the windows, I saw a well-lit room—the library. At this point I extracted my floor plan and studied it again, crouched in the shadows. Above the library was a terrace with a stone railing that let out from a guest bedroom suite. Looking up, I saw that all the bedroom windows were dark. Given that the safe was in the library, it might be my best means of entry.

I looked into the library again. A servant had walked in and was serving tea to a person or people I couldn't see. Should I wait until the library was vacant, or enter the house now and hide from within? I decided to enter now. I was becoming cold, and the bedroom would probably be inhabited later anyway. And it would be foolish to enter the library itself from outside even after it had been vacated, since there was almost certainly a video monitor inside.

But how to get to the terrace? I moved a little farther, careful to look for trip wires, and spotted a drainpipe at the rear corner of the house. Looking around and seeing no one, I shot across the lawn, keeping low to the ground until I reached the wall. I flattened myself against it and once more searched for guards. A patrol seemed to be approaching the front corner of the house opposite me; I could hear footsteps and hushed voices. Immediately I gripped the drainpipe and pulled myself up, bit by bit, until I had reached the top. I threw myself over the railing just as the guards appeared. Heart pounding, I sank against the ornate balustrade and waited for them to pass. Another moment and they would have seen me.

I now looked at the bedroom windows. They were still dark, so I crept across the terrace toward them, taking care that my footsteps should not be heard in the library below. When I reached the first window, I tried to pull it open. It was locked or stuck, so I moved past the bedroom door and tried the other. It, too, was locked.

Finally I tried the door. It was not only locked, but I noticed the telltale strips of alarm tape on its windows. The door would not be a good idea.

I moved back to the first window, which was toward the rear of the house. I removed the glass cutters from my backpack and cut a hole just above the place where I assumed the lock would be. After removing the glass, I reached in and found a catch, which I tripped open. The window slid smoothly upward. I had gained access to the house.

I slipped inside and closed the window. I fitted the missing glass precariously into its hole, where it seemed reasonably stable. I then took stock of my surroundings.

I could see little except that the bedroom was empty. There was a plush four-poster bed against one wall, and a fireplace with an ornate mantel as well. Velvet drapes hung from the ceiling. It was difficult to tell whether the bedroom was in use or not. There were three doorways, which led to a closet, a bathroom, and main second-floor hallway. This last door was slightly ajar, and I peered through the crack outside. The hallway was well lit, extending some sixty or seventy feet to the other side of the house. Halfway in between was the top of the stairway. I pushed the door open a few more inches, trying to recall the floor plan. There were two bedroom doors immediately outside, one on each side of the hallway, and another pair twenty feet farther. Then came the stairway and five more doors, two on each side and one, directly opposite me, at the end.

I shut the door and glanced at my watch. It was 2200 hours;

51

by midnight the embassy personnel would probably be in bed. In the meantime I would just have to wait.

I opened the door to the closet and switched on my flashlight. It was huge inside, and filled with evening gowns and western-style suits. I moved to the rear and settled myself behind a curtain of expensive fabric, turning off my flashlight. If the room was indeed occupied, then I would have to wait for its occupants to fall asleep before moving downstairs. I couldn't find a better hiding place for now, since moving through the hallway would be too risky.

An hour passed. I was struck by a faint sense of absurdity at the whole situation. Here I was, a woman in my early twenties, stalking through a mock embassy to pass a Foreign Intelligence test! It seemed so far removed from the ordinary life I had once known, from my mother and her home-cooked meals, my father relaxing in his easy chair after dinner, my garrulous brothers and sister. What were they doing at this moment? Were they in turn, perhaps, thinking about me?

My thoughts were interrupted as the bedroom door opened and the light was turned on. I heard footsteps and voices—a man's and a woman's. They were speaking in Japanese, though I couldn't make out their exact words. I became tense, heart pounding, and tried to retreat farther into the closet, my AK-47 bumping against the wall. The woman's voice became louder, and abruptly the closet light was switched. Even behind my clothes my eyes were smarting. The woman laughed, saying something, or so I thought, about the misery of living in Cairo for six months. The hangers slid toward me, and I felt the clothes pressed against me. There was a rustling sound as the woman removed her dress, which she then hung up. She then seemed to take something else from another hanger and suddenly the light was switched off again, leaving me in darkness. Her voice receded. I wondered if the man would follow in turn, but as the minutes passed, it appeared as though he wouldn't. I could vaguely perceive the bedroom light extinguish, and a few moments later there was silence.

My pulse continued to race. I now would have to wait an additional half hour or so before going anywhere, to allow the couple a chance to get to sleep. I shut my eyes and leaned my head against the wall. It seemed as though I was doing a haphazard job at best, and yet what else could I do, considering my deadline? I could only deliberate so long before action became essential.

When a seemingly appreciable length of time had elapsed I cautiously parted the clothes and got to my feet. The closet door had been left ajar, and after listening for a moment I pushed it open. My eyes were now adjusted to the darkness, and I could clearly make out the bed only fifteen feet away. The two people were only vague shapes in the dimness, indistinct blurs. The man was snoring deeply. I crept across the carpet toward the hall door.

Suddenly there was a gasp. I spun around and saw the woman sitting up in bed. A moment later a light was turned on, and I blinked painfully in the unwelcome glare.

"Shut up!" I snapped in Japanese, moving toward her, a pistol drawn. She was a middle-aged Asian woman with a fancy Western perm. She wore an apricot nightgown of a very expensive quality. Her mouth was open, and her hands were pressed against her face. When I was a few feet away, she smiled suddenly and lowered her hands.

"It's all right," she said in Korean. "At this point we're either dead or unconscious. Consider us eliminated."

I paused uncertainly. "Don't worry, Ok Hwa," she continued soothingly. "We expected you sooner or later. I'm impressed that you didn't shoot me."

I smiled beneath my mask. "I hope you'll at least turn the light out and keep quiet?"

"Of course," she replied. "Good luck!"

The man had been snoring throughout this episode and gave no sign of having heard any of this. I lowered the gun and walked to the door. The light was extinguished.

I slipped into the hallway. Only a few dim night-lights had been left on. I stole across the floor to the stairway, which swept down to the first level in a wide curve. The steps were marble, but my shoes were soft-soled and made little sound. Pistol ready, I padded downstairs into a large antechamber, straight into a guard seated at a desk near the front door.

We spotted each other at the same time, but before he could move, I had brought up the pistol and emptied a few shots at him. The paint pellets splattered over his shirtfront and left cheek, and a moment later he grinned at me and keeled over.

At the bottom of the stairs I looked around. Dimly lit hall-ways branched to the left and right, each lined with doors. At the end of the left hallway was the library, whose door was shut. I could see no light from under the door, so I assumed the room was empty. At that point I looked up and found a sur-veillance camera panning across the room toward me. Instantly I dived beneath its line of sight and rolled toward the wall, noting an electric eye in the wall a few feet above me when I stopped. My heart began to pound all over again. I was not being methodical enough, and my next mistake might be the last. When the camera had panned in the other direction, I stood and darted into the hallway toward the library. The door was locked, and I fumbled for a pick. It was a long minute before I could jimmy the door and slip inside, closing the door after me.

I switched on my flashlight. The safe was supposed to be behind a painting near the door. I played the beam across the walls until I came to a watercolor landscape that seemed to fit the bill. I removed the painting, and sure enough, there was the safe.

I set down my pack and withdrew the stethoscope, which I applied to the door of the safe. I turned the dial, listening to the tumblers, pulling whenever I heard a telltale click. A minute later and the safe was opened.

I reached inside and found a single sheet of paper. I snatched it up and pored over it.

"Ok Hwa," it said in Japanese, "you are halfway to the fin-ish! When you meet Instructor Rae Hong this morning, you are to repeat these exact words to him as best you can. Good luck."

I felt a thrill of elation as I replaced the paper and closed the safe, spinning the dial so that it locked. I replaced the painting. I might just succeed with this crazy assignment after all.

At that point I heard the crunching of gravel and looked up to see a military jeep approaching the embassy at high speed. Shocked, I switched off my flashlight and ran to the window. How could they know already?

And then it struck me. I had avoided the camera, but the guard's inert body certainly had not.

The jeep braked to a screeching halt, and two men jumped

out. I heard the front door opening and was jolted into action. I had to get out of here now.

Quickly I tried the windows. They were all locked and in fact seemed painted shut, and I could not break the wooden frames. The only way out was the hallway I'd just come from.

I heard footsteps pounding down the hallway already, and a moment later the door burst open. I dropped into a crouch, waiting. The room was dark, and they couldn't see me yet. I held my pistol ready.

Suddenly the light was flicked on. At once I squeezed a few shots off, striking the two guards who were poised outside. They dropped their guns and sank to the floor, covered with red paint. I stood and rushed past them, jamming another clip into my pistol as I ran.

I remembered the presence of the electric eye in the ante-chamber and rolled under its sight, but I needn't have bothered. The two guards had obviously alerted the whole place to my presence, because I heard footsteps upstairs and voices shouting outside. I burst out the front door and sprinted across the terrace toward the lawn. The gates would surely still be guarded, and my only hope was to escape the way I had come in, scaling the wall in some other place. But I'd only gone a few yards when a patrol rounded the corner of the house, three strong. The guards dropped to the ground, rolling onto their stomachs with machine guns at the ready. I retreated behind a Doric column as a chorus of paint pellets struck the stone next to me. I unslung the AK-47 with one hand and fired a volley in their direction, still holding the pistol in my other hand. I then dashed across the terrace, releasing sporadic bursts at them, and I heard a cry of surprise and pain. I must have gotten one of them! At the end of the terrace I vaulted over the railing and hit the lawn running. Two guards were charging in pursuit, firing their machine guns, and a few pellets struck the ground near my feet. I turned and, still running, emptied the rest of the AK-47's clip at them. I missed, but they were obliged to hit the ground, which bought me some time. I reached the wall, which threw a big shadow across the lawn, and ran along its length for a time, trusting the darkness to hide me. Finally I stopped and reloaded the AK-47. I then took out the rope and threw it over the wall and pulled until the grappling hook caught. I placed the AK-47 and pack on my shoulders. And then I heard something that made my blood freeze: the frenzied, ceaseless barking of what sounded like very angry dogs.

They had been released from the house. And they were drawing nearer.

Terrified, I began scaling the wall. My arms felt weak and rubbery because of my fear, and my feet slipped against the stone. There was a shout; I had been seen. The dogs were closing in steadily. Desperately I pulled myself to the top of the wall, gasping, and threw myself to the other side, landing heavily. A moment later I heard the dogs barking from the spot I'd just been.

I took a moment to catch my breath before running along the wall toward the pine forest. I had a pistol in my right hand, and I was waiting for the first sign of a guard. Sure enough, when I was thirty feet from the southeast corner, another patrol lurched into view. With a shout I emptied seven or eight rounds at them, not checking my pace. They tried to retreat, but I continued shooting until the clip was empty and the guards were lying in a heap and thoroughly covered with paint.

"Well done!" I heard as I passed them.

I charged into the forest, gripping the flashlight with my free hand and switching it on. I felt as though my heart burst, and I knew that it was essential that I stop to rest, but I wanted to put some distance between myself and the compound first. Though reluctant to use the flashlight, I had no alternative. I would run into a tree within seconds otherwise.

When I had covered a hundred yards, I stopped. I sank against a tree trunk and turned off my flashlight. I had never been so out of breath in my entire life, and my pulse was like a jackjammer in my chest and throat. Dazedly I reloaded the pistol, wondering how long it would be before I could continue.

I didn't have long to decide. I could soon hear the distant sound of barking again, and intuitively I guessed that they were putting the dogs on my trail.

I staggered to my feet and pushed on. The dogs would be kept on leads and could therefore move only as fast as my human pursuers. I switched on my flashlight again, dodging among the tree trunks. It would still be a few minutes before they picked up my scent—time enough to lose them, provided I did everything correctly.

A quarter of a mile farther on I came across a brook, no more than three or four feet wide. I plunged into it and waded upstream, my feet recoiling from the icy coldness of the water. When I had followed the course for a few hundred feet, I leaped onto the bank and continued through the forest. Now I was searching for a tree I could climb, and fortunately there are many such trees in a pine forest.

Five minutes later I was perched atop an enormous larch tree. I could still hear the barking in the distance, and even see the flickering flashlights; but my pursuers, if indeed they'd found my trail, seemed to have lost it at the brook. As I waited, catching my breath, they moved off toward the compound. They were calling it off.

I sighed in relief and even cried for a few minutes. I was utterly exhausted and psychologically drained. I looked at my watch— 0220 hours. I still had several miles to cover, and less than four hours in which to do so. I descended from the tree and took out my compass and flashlight. It was time to move on.

I moved mechanically, putting one foot in front of the other by force of habit. I had been covered in sweat, and now I felt cold and clammy in the chill night air. I did not think about anything in particular, and I no longer felt a sense of urgency. My mind was blank. I could only dully proceed and trust that I would soon reach the camp.

It was 0500 hours when I finally came to the Keumsung Mountain trail. My legs, particularly my knees and ankles, were throbbing with pain, and I was beginning to feel feverish. I shuffled on, descending along the trail until I had reached the courtyard. I was nearly sobbing with relief at this point, longing only to get into my bed and sleep for the next day or two. I opened the door to my house and stumbled inside.

Rae Hong and Myung were waiting inside, dozing on the sofa. They stirred and woke when I entered, and their eyes widened in expectation.

A day later, when all the reports had been analyzed, it was determined that I would receive 98 points for the field test, one of the highest scores on record. The only thing that had kept me from a perfect score was the fact that I had been forced to shoot so many guards and had caused a ruckus in general.

But at that moment I could only repeat, like a robot, the words that had somehow become etched in my mind a few hours earlier: "Ok Hwa, you are halfway to the finish! When you meet Inspector Rae Hong this morning, you are to repeat these exact words to him as best you can. Good luck."

The last thing I noticed, as I sank to the floor and passed out, was Rae Hong's smile.

CHAPTER FIVE

IN THE YEARS between my recruitment as an intelligence agent and the bombing of Flight 858 I was given two major assignments, which were to be the preliminary tests of my abilities as an international spy.

In July 1984, by which time I had become an expert in both armed and unarmed combat, I was visited one day by Special Agent Chung, who arrived early in the morning in his black Mercedes. It was a Sunday, so I had the day off, and I was relaxing in the library with Volume 26 of *Selected Writings of Kim Il Sung*. Chung was shown in by Wul Chi, and I was so startled by his sudden appearance that I literally jumped out of my chair.

"Comrade Ok Hwa," he greeted me affably, offering his hand. "It's good to see you again. I understand you've been doing quite well here."

"Thank you, sir," I replied, accepting his hand.

"I want you to have your bags packed in fifteen minutes," he continued. "Just a few clothes, nothing more. Meet me outside when you're done."

"Of course," I said, trying unsuccessfully to hide my apprehension and surprise. "I'll be right there."

A short time later the Mercedes was threading its way along the mountain road. Chung asked a few polite questions about how I was doing, but would volunteer no details as to where we were going or why. I found myself wondering if I was being expelled from the camp and deported—a not unusual fear for any North Korean who is abruptly visited by a Party official. But despite his reticence Chung seemed in a good mood, and I began to doubt that I was being arrested.

We reached Intelligence Headquarters, and I was shown into the office of Department Chief Kwang. Kwang was a tall young man, prematurely balding, who, despite the fact that we were indoors, was wearing a pair of sunglasses. Also in his office was a short, elderly man with longish white hair and a face like crumpled parchment. They both stood as we entered, the old man doing so with obvious difficulty.

Chief Kwang introduced him to me as Kim Seung Il, "one of the most distinguished special agents in the history of Foreign Intelligence. Treat him as you would your own grandfather, Ok Hwa. You're going to be spending a lot of time together."

Once we were all seated, Kwang began to explain the reason for this meeting. "Mr. Kim, Miss Kim, you're going to be traveling abroad for the next month or so. For you, Ok Hwa, the purpose will be to gain experience in the field. You'll be traveling to many cities in Europe and Asia, and I want you to have some practice moving from country to country undercover. It's time you had some exposure to other cultures, and I want you to take careful notes during your journey. It will be an ideal chance to show that we can trust you in the coming years with top-secret missions.

"You'll be traveling as Japanese father and daughter. Both of you are proficient in the Japanese language, and your being tourists will provide an ideal cover as you move through Europe. You'll visit Moscow, Budapest, Vienna, Copenhagen, Frankfurt, Zurich, Geneva, Paris, Macao, Guangzhou, and Beijing. In the communist countries you'll use North Korean ambassadors' passports, but in the Western countries you'll use false Japanese passports with the names of Shinichi and Mayumi Hachiya. Shinichi will be the vice president of Ohoi

60

Transportation, and Mayumi will be a graduate of Yaoyama Women's College with a degree in Domestic Science. Complete details will be included in the dossiers that we shall give you, but for now these are the essentials.

"Ok Hwa, I should mention that you'll be traveling the last leg of the journey alone. When you leave Europe for China, Seung Il will remain behind for a day before flying alone to Seoul, where he will complete a mission of his own. Your trip to China will serve as both a diversion for anyone who may take an interest in the two of you as well as a test to determine if you can be relied upon to travel alone."

I listened to his words, feeling myself grow more and more excited. At last, after what felt like endless years of training, I was to be sent into the field! There were trainee agents at Keum-sung who waited ten or fifteen years for their first assignments, and I had waited only four. Needless to say, I also felt over-whelmed with awe and worry at this great responsibility with which they were entrusting me. My last and only trip abroad had been to Cuba, and most North Koreans never left the coun-try at all. All the details that the journey would entail—airports, hotels, money changing—seemed like more than I could cope with. Not to mention the fact that we would be entering the Western countries illegally as enemy spies.

It was actually a few weeks before the final arrangements for the trip were completed, during which I studied Japanese fash-ion magazines and films so that my dress, makeup, and basic mannerisms would be entirely authentic. I was also required to read a series of international travel guides. Absorbing all this information made me feel confident and sophisticated. I began to feel that I was on my way to becoming a master spy, like the legendary KGB and North Korean agents whom we had learned about in films. I was filled with pride. While most women my age could only look forward to becoming house-wives, I would be traveling the world. Little did I know that I would feel so differently in the years to come.

The European leg of the journey now seems like a blur. What were my impressions of my first glimpses of capitalist coun-tries? I was struck by that fact that the cities were generally clean, the establishments well serviced. Most of all, of course, I was astounded by the abundance and variety of goods that were available in the shops. Although the presence of luxury items, such as jewelry, was entirely foreign to me, it was the variety of food that surprised me the most. There was so *much* of it!

Truthfully, however, I nonetheless maintained my ingrained belief that the cities of Europe were corrupt, decadent, and inferior. In Copenhagen and Paris I was repelled by the abundance of pornography shops and the frequent appearance of prostitutes. In Switzerland I was disgusted by what seemed to be the flauntings of absurdly wealthy people—the mink coats, the Daimler limousines, the diamond earrings. But I had been raised for twenty-two years to believe that everything about the West was evil, so I was seeing this new world through well-programmed eyes.

What also prevented me from appreciating these cities was our disguise. Traveling abroad was in itself strange and confusing, intimidating even, but I was always preoccupied with my need to playact, to play the role of someone I was not. Although Seung Il and I visited all the major tourist attractions, as indeed we were required to in order to maintain our cover, I couldn't help but feel anxious at the sight of a policeman. Especially disconcerting was the profusion of Japanese tourists, some of whom would try to engage us in conversation. I felt therefore an undercurrent of tension throughout the trip.

But I could not fail to be impressed by Europe's beauty. Switzerland in particular was breathtaking. I fell in love with the Alps the moment I saw them, and our hotel on Lake Geneva seemed right out of a postcard. I remember that we encountered a group of Indian tourists near the hotel who were touching the snow in wonder, as they had never seen it before.

We had been given ten thousand dollars to cover our expenses, and it was expected that we would bring gifts back to North Korea for our departmental superiors as well as for our president. This was standard practice, I learned, among field agents, to show their honor at being sent abroad. The gifts were unremarkable by Western standards—they tended to be practical things like ballpoint pens and cigarette lighters, which were scarce in North Korea. Technically we were not allowed to spend any money on ourselves, except as needed to carry out our assignment, but Mr. Kim bought himself an expensive gold-plated watch anyway. Watches were a prized commodity in North Korea, and to own one was a mark of respect. Kim would later tell me that his family considered it to be the finest purchase he had ever made.

I myself had a longing to buy a small mermaid statue in Geneva, but since the mermaid's torso was bare, I knew that I could never have brought it back to Pyongyang. Instead I bought a necklace with a gold cross hanging from the end. Its symbolism meant nothing to me, but Seung Il, though he said nothing, glared at me when he saw me wear it. Interestingly, though, I was commended for it by Chief Kwang upon my return. He considered it perfect as part of my disguise. I of course refrained from mentioning that I had bought it purely for pleasure.

I must admit that some of my "professionalism" as an agent, if indeed I'd had any to begin with, sort of faded away in Switzerland. The landscape had a fairy-tale quality, and I did not want to leave.

In Paris Kim and I were to go our separate ways, but we did spend a few days together in our tourist disguises. I was impressed by certain things about Paris, particularly the chic of its women. I was amazed to note that middle-aged women dressed as daringly as twenty-year-olds. I also admired the grandeur of the old buildings. These pleasures were offset, however, when my purse was snatched by a motorcycle rider as I was crossing a street. Not to mention the incident when a Parisian cabbie cheated us by running up a hundred-dollar fare because of our ignorance.

Seung Il was a perfect gentleman throughout the trip. Although we stayed in the same hotel room, he never once made a pass at me or even suggestive comments. I had been apprehensive about this before the journey and had resolved to utilize my martial arts skills and beat him senseless at the first impropriety. Seung Il was a veteran agent, but he was old, and I did not doubt that I could handle him if I had to. But contrary to my fears he turned out to be like a real father to me. It was a great comfort, as I undertook this first assignment, to be in the company of a distinguished and experienced agent who could reassure me when I became too anxious about the plausibility of our disguise. He had been to Europe many times and possessed the kind of self-confidence that comes only with experience.

Although we had been instructed not to divulge our personal histories, it was impossible that we not learn something about our respective lives. Seung Il was married and had several grown children, and had been in Foreign Intelligence for longer than he cared to remember. His previous assignments had taken him all over the world, even to America. I sensed that he was a kind man beneath his frail but rugged exterior, though of course he had probably killed more than a few people in his lifetime in battling for communism. He was somewhere in his late sixties and suffered from chronic stomach problems. I think that after a while we cared for each other more than professionally. I think we became concerned about each other's personal welfare as family members do.

When it was time to leave Paris, Kim accompanied me to De Gaulle Airport for my departure to Macao. Though I was afraid to be left on my own, I forced myself not to show it. I didn't want anything about a sniveling young woman showing up in Kim's report when we returned.

"Be careful, Ok Hwa," he said, as we came to the security checkpoint where he could accompany me no farther. "Agent Chung will meet you in Macao and help you go on to Guangzhou. Tell him that I'll meet him on September twenty-sixth."

"Good luck, Seung Il," I answered, embracing him. "Will we meet again?"

He laughed. "I'm supposed to be retired," he said. "But nevertheless I certainly hope so."

We of course would be reunited later, but for a mission of far deadlier consequences.

In later years I would discover that Kim Seung Il, after he'd left me, had barely escaped from South Korea with his life. His contact in Seoul had been flushed out only minutes before their scheduled rendezvous. The contact, closely pursued by South Korean agents and police, managed to run into a beauty parlor and shoot himself before he could be apprehended. Seung Il had of course fled Seoul immediately, but had barely managed to get out before the authorities blocked every major road out of the city. Apparently the South Koreans had found out about him, and there was an uproar in Pyongyang as to whether we had a mole in Foreign Intelligence.

But meanwhile, in Macao, I knew nothing of this and went ahead trying to fulfill my own assignment. I was met by Agent Chung at the airport, and he spent a few days showing me around the island. He mentioned that I might later be assigned to Macao if everything went well, and to observe my surroundings closely. It was a capitalist mecca like Hong Kong, full of casinos and expensive hotels, but since it was Asian, it felt less unfamiliar to me than Europe had.

My real trepidation began when Chung saw me off to Guangzhou by train. Now for the next week I would truly be alone.

Fortunately, though, China was not as strange as I'd feared. It was, after all, a neighbor of North Korea, and communist as well. I was curious to observe how ordinary people lived in China and was both encouraged and depressed to discover that they lived better than North Koreans. It seemed to me that North Korea was the poorest country on earth. In China the shops were at least fully stocked and the restaurants were cheap and well serviced.

I stayed in Guangzhou for two days before moving on to Beijing. It was a crowded city, whose primary means of transportation was the bicycle. There seemed to be millions of them. Again I observed the way of life closely, and while the standard of living was not nearly as high as in Europe, it was still far superior to Pyongyang. Food seemed more plentiful, and smaller luxury items were readily available on the black market. I felt ashamed of my country.

As I left Beijing, I bought some gifts for the Pyongyang officials at the duty-free shop at the train station—five boxes of herbal medicine bottles, two bottles of cognac, and a box of pencils. I came to feel that it really was a strange country I lived in.

Perhaps the most telling thing about the trip to Europe was my evaluation, which I was required to submit to my superiors and which in retrospect seems absurd to me:

My visit to the capitalist countries of Europe only confirms what I had been taught about them. It was the exact truth that only a handful live well and that ordinary citizens lead awful lives. It was pure hell.

In contrast to the glittering streets of bright neon lights, there are back alleys where people live like animals.

I have seen fancy restaurants that are frequented only by capitalist pigs who have sucked the blood and sweat of the masses. The sight of their dogs, which are dressed better than ordinary people, is a sad and disgusting reflection of their failed society.

I feel very proud that the citizens of North Korea live, work, and study together and do not have to worry about their daily needs. My resolution to devote my life to our socialist utopia and protect her from our enemies is now greater than ever.

It is an honor and a privilege to serve the Great Leader in my appointed role, and I am forever grateful that I have been fortunate enough to be born in North Korea.

I was also required to write an evaluation of my own performance and that of Kim Seung Il. Agents were required to observe each other as much as their surroundings, and it would have been unthinkable not to include plenty of self-criticism about myself and Seung Il.

Needless to say, I had trouble finding the words.

CHAPTER SIX

AFTER ANY TRIP abroad a special agent is required to undergo a three-month ideological course to reaffirm his or her commitment to socialist ideals. Surprisingly, to me at any rate, I couldn't wholly discredit or forget the affluent and carefree societies I had left behind in Europe. Memories of the well-stocked shops and beautifully dressed people kept coming back to me.

Sook Hee was jealous of my assignment but was happy to see me again. We were soon talking like old friends, and I, too, was glad to be back with her. I was not supposed to talk about the trip with anyone, but I found it impossible not to tell her at least where I had been.

I now had to take up studies in Chinese, since a new requirement had been implemented that every agent learn three foreign languages. Several months later Sook Hee and I were told that we were to be stationed in Guangzhou to learn the language more thoroughly, to be followed by a six-month stint in Macao. We were thrilled to be going abroad and even more so that this time we would be able to stay together.

In Guangzhou we stayed at the house of Agent Park Chang

Rae, who helped us with the intricacies of the Cantonese dialect and to blend in with Chinese society. It was fantastically hot—a hundred degrees—and the streets were packed with people. Every Saturday Chang Rae would conduct a review of our week's work to be certain that we were progressing well.

It was a happy year. We had a fair bit of personal liberty, our host was kind and considerate, and we had many opportunities to meet interesting people. It was the first time we were really on our own. Sook Hee and I became even closer and spoke more intimately about our childhoods than our superiors would have liked.

Sook Hee wanted someday to marry. I myself was ambivalent about marriage and hadn't thought about it a great deal, since the Party came first. But then again, my career also seemed to be advancing more quickly than hers. Sook Hee was bright but not exceptionally so, and her engaging good looks had probably been the major factor in her selection to the Agency. She was more domestically inclined than I, dreaming of having children, of running a household. And she was at times less than discreet about her criticism of North Korea.

"Even in China they live so much better than us," she complained to me one evening as we lay sweating in our beds from the summer humidity. "What was it like in Europe, Ok Hwa? Please tell me."

"You know I shouldn't."

"Oh, come on. Who's to know?"

I thought for a while, feeling torn. "Well, it's not perfect in the West—far from it. There are things you'd never dream of having in North Korea—prostitutes, robberies, murders, beggars in the streets. Still, I do miss it in a way. But what's the good of talking? We're stuck here."

"If I'm ever sent to Europe, I'm going to defect," she said.

I was shocked. "Sook Hee!"

"No, really. I've heard the stories, Ok Hwa. There's ten times as much food, everybody has a car, and you can choose whatever career you want."

I felt confused and a little angry at her, and I didn't know what to say. What she said was true, but there was no point in encouraging her.

"I want to marry a European—a blond one preferably. I want

to live in my own house. I don't need to be rich. I just want to be . . . *free.*"

Her outburst made me worry for her. "Sook Hee, the fact is we're living in a country that is still developing. One day North Koreans will enjoy all those same luxuries, only everyone will have an equal stake, not just the rich. And anyway, you'd better watch what you say. If any Party official heard you speak those words, you'd get the club."

Whatever she or I had experienced in our training or in China could not have prepared us for Macao.

There we actually lived by ourselves in a capitalist society. We had an apartment and a bank account. We paid bills and bought groceries. We visited nightclubs to absorb the local culture. Everything was dazzlingly new to us, and it was also a lot of fun.

I had learned hardly anything about Macao during my first short trip there, but I soon became familiar with its day-to-day life. We did not make friends, because our orders were to keep to ourselves. We were not there as tourists; our orders were to practice our Cantonese and improve our abilities to impersonate Chinese nationals. There was a good chance that we were being watched by North Korean agents, so we were always on our guard.

But this took enormous discipline, which we sometimes lacked. In nightclubs Sook Hee spent most of the time on the dance floor with local businessmen, and more than once I had to drag her away. Again and again I was propositioned, and because I was extremely shy, I never knew how to respond.

One night I was dancing with a wealthy financier from Hong Kong who clearly wanted to know me better. He was in his late thirties, dressed in an expensive suit, and asked me the usual pleasantries—where I was from, what I did, and so on. I felt myself becoming flustered. I didn't know what to reply. On impulse I grabbed Sook Hee, who was dancing provocatively with a Caucasian nearby, and pulled her out of the nightclub.

"What are you doing?" she snapped, yanking her hand away as we stepped outside.

"Sook Hee, I can't stand it! How can we pass for natives if we can't . . . *be* with them!"

"Why, Ok Hwa!" she said in mock surprise. "This is rather strange, coming from you, always the good girl."

"Everything's just so different here. I don't know what to say to men."

"You should say, 'Marry me, honey, and take me away from all this.' A few moments more with that Austrian and I would have done just that."

I stared at her in shock, all the more so because I felt inclined to agree with her. "Are you serious?"

Sook Hee fished for a cigarette. She'd picked up a smoking habit in the past few weeks, and demurely she took a long drag. "You're damn right I am."

Of course these encounters never amounted to anything, though I felt myself becoming increasingly drawn into this dynamic, capitalist culture. It was probably for my own good that we were soon recalled to Pyongyang.

I was permitted a visit home upon our return. I had bought a portable radio for my little brother, Bum Soo, and a few other gifts for my family. But when I arrived at our apartment, I found the mood to be somber.

Bum Soo had died.

When my mother told me the news, I dropped the radio on the floor and started to cry. I rushed over to hug her. Oh, poor Bum Soo! He had been such a wonderful little brother, always cheerful and laughing. Skin cancer had claimed his life at fifteen. My parents had been expecting it for some time, but still they were devastated. My father for some reason avoided me during this visit, though not because he was angry at me, as I was soon to learn.

It had been almost two years since my last visit, and during that period my sister, Hyun Ok, had been married to a travel guide at the Bureau of Tourism. I sensed that my mother was disappointed that I had not been the first one to marry. I also sensed that I was drifting farther and farther away from my family. I had been forbidden to talk about my training or my missions, so there was a sense of strain, of not knowing what to say. Oh, there were so many things that we wanted to tell each other! But instead we only became more and more estranged.

All the same, nothing could have prepared me for my father's behavior when Agent Chung dropped by a few days later to pick me up. When my mother opened the door to let him in, my father strode across the room and grabbed Chung by the neck, pushing him against the wall.

"When are you returning my daughter to me, damn you?" he yelled, tears streaming down his face. "When?!"

"Father," I said, alarmed, terrified, feeling that at all costs I had to stop him. "Let him go!" This sort of behavior could bring the firing squad down on all of us!

My father eased his grip. Chung seemed embarrassed and said he would wait for me in the car.

"Father—?" I said.

"Out!" he shouted, shoving me toward the door. "You're not my daughter anymore. You belong to them. So, go! Go back to them!"

CHAPTER SEVEN

FOR THE NEXT week I could not concentrate on my training. I went through the motions mechanically, and during the long marches I sometimes found myself stepping out of time. I could not get my mind off my family.

The death of Bum Soo had upset me greatly of course; but now I was thinking more about my parents. I was angry at my father for his behavior in front of Special Agent Chung, but deep down I felt for him and knew that he was right. Our family was now split apart, in all likelihood forever; and because he loved me, it was hard for him to let go.

That Saturday I made a decision. Sundays were our one free day, and we were free to spend them as we liked. There were no drills, no lessons, no roll calls; and if I could persuade Wul Chi not to report me, I might not be missed for a day.

When our training had finished for the day, and twilight had fallen on the camp, I sought out Wul Chi in the kitchen. She greeted me warmly as usual. Of all the camp personnel she was by far the most likable.

"Wul Chi, I must see my family," I said to her. "I want to leave tonight, when it's dark. I'll be back tomorrow evening. I plead for you to not report me when I don't show up for breakfast."

She looked at me in horror. "Ok Hwa, I'll be glad to keep your secret, but the supervisors can still find out. You know what'll happen if they do."

I did know of course. We were forbidden to leave the camp at any time, and if my absence was noticed and reported, I would immediately be deported to a labor camp in the far north for the rest of my life. I might even be shot. And my family would probably share a similar fate.

Yet I couldn't sit still. It could be years before I was granted another leave to go home, and I could not endure the thought of my parents waiting for so long with this painful matter unresolved between us. It had taken some time for the realization to hit me, but I now knew that my family was more important to me than the Party or the government. When I had first been chosen by the Party, I had been overflowing with pride. And yet when I thought back to my childhood, to the years of growing up in Cuba and Pyongyang, I knew that nothing was more important to me than my family. I was still proud to be chosen by the Party, and I would do anything for the reunification of North Korea. But I would no longer neglect the people I loved.

"There's nothing else I can do," I told Wul Chi. "My brother is dead, and my father is miserable. I must see him."

She sighed, and her face was full of concern. There was only so far that she could go to protect me, and much would be left to chance. "If you think it's best, then go," she said, taking my hand. "But be careful, Ok Hwa, please. I don't want anything bad to happen to you."

I squeezed her hand and went to my room. There I told Sook Hee about my intentions, and she expressed the same fearful reservations as Wul Chi.

"Look," I said. "The commander hardly ever comes around here on Sunday. And if he does, just say that I was gone when you woke up this morning and that you don't know where I am."

She nodded, but I could tell that she wasn't mollified. The thought had almost surely crossed her mind that she, too, could get in trouble if I went ahead with this. I sat on her bed and laid a hand on her knee. "They won't do anything to you, Sook

Hee," I said, hoping my words carried some weight. "Just say that you don't know a thing."

She looked away for a moment, sighing, and then she smiled and looked back. "Don't worry," she said. "My lips are sealed."

"Thanks." I leaned over and gave her a quick embrace and then stood to gather what I'd need for the trip. Since I'd be spending the night traveling, I wouldn't need clothes; and I couldn't afford to be hampered by a backpack anyway. I changed into the darkest outfit I owned and took some money and my identification card. I tied my hair back, out of my eyes, and then put on a black army cap and pulled the brim low.

I went to the window and looked out. It was entirely dark now, and there would be no point in delaying any further.

Sook Hee stood, and we hugged again. "Good luck," she said as we parted. "Be careful."

"Thanks. I will." I smiled and then slipped into the hallway and out into the night.

There was a security checkpoint at the entrance to the camp, which I would have to avoid by stealing through the woods, picking up the road somewhere beyond. But I would also have to contend with the foot soldiers who patrolled the camp's perimeter. These men would be armed with machine guns and they were accompanied by large black dogs. Heart pounding, I slipped into the pinewood that ringed the valley and set out in what I thought would be the right direction.

Fortunately there was little undergrowth in the forest, and a soft bed of pine needles covered the ground. The night was warm and clear, with a half-moon, but little moonlight could filter through the trees. It was almost pitch-black, and I was forced to grope my way from trunk to trunk. I thought wryly that my years of training were now being put to good use.

Bit by bit I proceeded about a hundred yards before I came to the fence that rimmed this side of the camp. I must have been about a quarter of a mile west of the gates—far enough to avoid notice. But I would have to get over the fence, and the top was lined with barbed wire.

I looked up, my eyes now used to the dark. The pine branches were black against a beautiful starry sky. The tree closest to me had some low branches, and I scrambled up until

I was above the top level of the fence. I then crawled along a branch that, though it did not overhang the barbed wire, seemed close enough that a jump might carry me over the fence.

When I had gone out on the limb as far as I could, I gripped the branch above me and pulled myself to my feet. I was about three feet above the barbed wire and perhaps three feet away from it, and roughly fifteen feet above the ground. It would be a long jump for a person of my size; but scared as I was, I was resolved to do it.

I took a deep breath and jumped.

I cleared the barbed wire with scant inches to spare and hit the ground hard. Forcing myself to ignore the pain in my legs, I rolled into a crouch and looked around. At that moment I heard footsteps and froze.

The terrain beyond the fence stretched into an open field, with tall, thick grass and some clumps of shrubbery. I hid myself within the folds of a big bush and waited, hardly daring to breathe.

A moment later a figure appeared, waving a flashlight across the ground. Beside him strode a large black dog. He must have heard me when I jumped, because he was pointing the flashlight into the tall grass around me. When he was a few feet away from me, he stopped, playing the beam in a wide arc. I flattened myself against the ground, and I could feel the beam only a foot or two above me. With my heart pounding like a drum, I prayed that the dog wouldn't smell me out.

He stood there for a long time, and I knew that if he spotted me, I would have to fight him, possibly even kill him if he saw my face. That way at least I could return to the camp and escape immediate punishment. It was possible that the commander would think that his death had resulted from an outside attack.

I tensed, holding my breath, and peered up at the tall figure not ten feet away. His face was dimly lit by the wide radius of the flashlight's beam, but I did not recognize him. I was prepared to spring at him immediately, hoping to knock him out before he could recognize me. Of course that would still leave the dog. And I had no idea what I would do about the dog.

But abruptly the patroller moved on, walking in the direction of the gates. I waited until he was out of sight before breathing an enormous sigh of relief.

When I was sure he was far enough away, I stood and began to make my way through the field. I headed northeast, at a forty-five-degree angle from the fence, expecting to pick up the road soon. I took care not to make any noise and was glad that my training had been so thorough. Compared with living for days in the open in a small foxhole, this seemed easy.

Fifteen minutes later I reached the road. From the cover of some bushes I looked in both directions, but it was empty. I slipped out into the open and began the long walk to the Pyongyang Road, which I knew was some ten miles away.

Because of the intensive conditioning I had undergone, I was able to keep a good pace. The night grew cooler, and there was a deep silence around me. The dark bulk of the mountains loomed in the moonlight, and I hoped with all my heart that I wouldn't run into a tiger. During my years at the various camps I had never encountered one personally, but occasionally on our long marches along mountain paths we would see their tracks in the dirt. There were rumors that someone in the village closest to the camp had been walking for exercise one evening and had been snatched away.

Hours passed; I did not stop. At one point I heard the engine of a car approaching behind me, and instantly I took cover. Moments later a Mercedes drove by, stirring up dust in its wake. I waited until the red taillights had vanished before proceeding.

I reached the Pyongyang Road shortly before dawn, when the sky had assumed a purplish hue and the air felt suddenly cold. I was sweating, and I began to shiver. Once I struck the main road, I turned south and continued my trek. After another two hours I reached the outskirts of a town.

By now it was light, and the town was beginning to awaken. I reached into a pocket and extracted a pair of sunglasses. Now that I was in the open, I would have to be even more careful.

At the town center there was a small bus station, where I learned that a single bus would be leaving within the hour for Pyongyang, arriving at mid-morning. And there would be a single bus returning in the late afternoon.

I was glad to be able to sit down and even dozed off as I

waited. A few of the townfolk came to wait for the bus as well.

At last the bus came, and we were headed for the city. The now-familiar countryside flashed by, the cultivated fields and pinewoods and mountains.

The bus dropped me only a few blocks from my family's new apartment. It was still only ten A.M., but I had only four hours to spare. The streets at this hour were relatively empty, and I was relieved that no one was around to notice me.

I reached the apartment building and mounted the steps that led to my family's unit. Outside the door I knocked and waited.

My mother answered, and immediately her face assumed a shocked expression. But then she recovered and swept me into her arms. "Hyun Hee," she whispered, holding me tightly. "What are you doing here? Where is Mr. Chung?" Without waiting for an answer, she released me and strode into the apartment, calling to my father and brother. "Our Hyun Hee is back!"

My father wandered in from the bedroom he shared with my mother. His face had a tired, worn expression, but he brightened immediately when he saw me.

As though no time had elapsed since our last meeting, I shouted the first words that came to my mind. "What have I done wrong?"

He seemed taken aback by my anger. He could not hold my gaze, and shuffled over to a chair. When he had seated himself, he said, "You have done nothing wrong, Hyun Hee. I'm only having some trouble accepting your new position and detaching my feelings from you."

His voice was full of sadness, and I felt my anger evaporate. "What do you mean?"

"You belong to the Party now," he replied, at last meeting my gaze. "Biologically of course you are still our daughter, and in our hearts this will always be so. But it would be foolish not to acknowledge that, practically speaking, you are now the Party's daughter, not ours." He gave a thin smile, as though at some private joke. "Naturally your mother and I are honored by your having been chosen by the Party, but I'm afraid that doesn't make it much easier for us emotionally. We love you, Hyun Hee, and now we'll see you only rarely for the rest of our lives. When we were younger, your mother and I had dreams that you would find a good husband and live nearby and that we could enjoy our grandchildren. This will not happen. And now that Hyun Ok is a widow, and"—he sighed—"well, it's difficult."

I felt tears running down my cheeks. I was ashamed at my previous anger for him, and once again I felt as though by joining the Party I had betrayed my family. Looking back, I cannot help but feel a deep sense of resentment toward the North Korean government. To them we as individuals were as nothing; all sense of our humanity was sacrificed to some abstract concept of "socialism," "the Party," "the collective good." Why else did we address each other as "comrade," as the first Marxist-Leninists had, discouraging any hint of intimacy?

And this was the price I was paying. I was a privileged member of the elite now, a full-fledged Party member, the dream of every North Korean. It was a bit like being a priest—it might be a high calling, but there was a terrible price to pay for it.

I spent the next few hours with my family, looking through old photo albums and talking about the future. It was out of the question, at least for the moment, that I resign from the Party; this would only have brought disgrace upon my whole family. But I knew that I would wither away if I had to spend the rest of my life in a training camp; and it was not unheard of for some agents, after completing a particularly dangerous mission, to be placed in retirement and allowed to return to their families.

My mother, as usual, cooked an enormous dinner for me. The atmosphere of the house lightened somewhat, and my father seemed to have returned to normal, but my mother's face was set in a dour expression, and I knew that she, even more than my father, hated to see me leave.

After a tearful farewell I was walking down the street toward the bus stop. I felt emotionally drained but also a sense of relief. I was glad that I had returned home. Things felt as right as they could be, at least for now.

I dozed on the bus. I was starting to feel the exhaustion from the previous night. When we finally reached the town that was near the camp, I barely woke in time to disembark. My legs and feet were sore, but there was nothing I could do except go on.

As I walked, I began to wonder if I had been missed during the day. But if I had, surely they would have already come after me and arrested me? Then again, it was possible that they would wait in their own time for me to return and arrest me at their convenience. Grimly I pushed on, ignoring the pain. The clear sky of the morning had given way to a bank of gray clouds.

Toward dusk it began to rain, and within minutes I was thoroughly soaked. Twice I heard cars approaching and twice I was forced to take cover in the bushes that flanked the road. An enormous blister on my right foot had opened, and each step brought excruciating pain. The rain, which had started in a ferocious downpour, now settled into a steady rhythm. I knew that it would not soon abate.

About eight o'clock I could see the security checkpoint in the distance, and I slipped off the road into the field. Because of the gray skies overhead, it did not seem fully dark, and I was forced at times to crawl through the field to remain concealed. The ground had turned into a bog, and my clothes became spattered with mud. By now I was so tired that I was moving by sheer habit, mechanically placing one foot in front of the other. I could think only of returning to my room and taking a long, hot bath.

When I neared the fence, I paused, looking in all directions. There did not seem to be any guards in the vicinity, so I rose from a crouch and began to climb the fence. I hadn't given any thought to the fact that I would have no trees to help me with the fence and that I would just have to take my chances with the barbed wire. As I reached the top, I gripped the vertical fencepost next to me, which tapered inward, toward the camp, and climbed until my feet were planted in the top links of the fence. Taking a deep breath, I pushed off with my feet and into a handstand, and threw my legs toward the interior of the camp while simultaneously pushing off with my hands. I flipped over in the air and cleared the barbed wire, but I overcompensated my somersault and landed on my hands and knees in a puddle of rainwater. Miraculously I wasn't hurt, but it was a long moment before I recovered my strength and was able to continue.

I crept through the pinewoods, aiming toward the lights I

could see through the trees, and I soon reached the outskirts of the camp. There was no one around, thankfully, and I jogged toward the front door of the lodge and let myself in. I felt so relieved, I wanted to shout and scream.

Sook Hee was reading in our bedroom and looked up as I came in. She immediately burst out laughing and clapped her hands together.

"What the hell is so funny?" I growled, stripping off my clothes.

She covered her mouth with one hand, but only laughed harder. "If you could see yourself," she wheezed.

Irritated, I strode toward the mirror that was mounted on the door, and I started to giggle myself. My cheeks were smeared with mud, and my hair had come loose from the cap and was straggling down across my face. "Look," I said, removing the last of my clothes and wrapping a towel around myself, "did anyone find out about me?"

She stopped laughing, but a smile remained on her face. "Don't worry, you're safe. It's been dead around here all day. So tell me how it was."

"Oh, Sook Hee, I can't explain. It's . . . difficult. I sometimes wonder what I'm doing here."

I took a long bath, savoring the hot water as it penetrated my skin. My fatigue and the balminess of the steam almost made me doze off again. Languidly I stood, stepped out of the tub, and dried myself off. I returned to my bedroom in something of a daze, only to find Sook Hee pacing the room with an urgent expression on her face.

"Ok Hwa," she said as I came inside. "You're back not a moment too soon. Special Agent Chung has just arrived here and is waiting for you in the living room."

"Chung?" I said, panic rising in me. "He didn't find out, did he?"

"No, no, nothing like that," she said. "At least I don't think so. I think it's something about a mission. There's an old man with him, a Kim Seung Il."

"Kim Seung Il?"

She nodded. "Come on, get dressed. I told them you wouldn't be long."

My mind racing, I quickly slipped into some clean clothes,

dragged a comb through my hair, and half ran to the living room. Mr. Chung was sitting at the table at the far end talking to Kim Seung Il. They stood as I came into the room.

"Ok Hwa," said Chung, smiling. "You remember Mr. Kim here?"

I gave a short bow. "Of course. It's good to see you again, Seung Il. Do sit down."

We seated ourselves. Chung fumbled in his pockets for a cigarette, offered one to Kim, and they both lit up. "Well," said Chung, exhaling as he spoke. "No doubt you're wondering why we're here on such a night. I'm not at liberty to say anything just yet, but I wonder if you could be ready to leave here in fifteen minutes?"

"Leave?" I said, surprised. "Of course. But where? For how long?"

"Let me start with your second question," replied Chung. "You should pack everything you own, because it's unlikely that you'll be coming back." For a moment I felt my blood turn to ice. I thought that he had learned of my "free act," as we called leaving the camp unpermitted, and was politely arresting me. But my fear diminished as he continued. "As to your first question, suffice it to say that we're going to Pyongyang, to Intelligence Headquarters. You've been given a mission."

CHAPTER EIGHT

THE MERCEDES GLIDED smoothly through the empty streets of Pyongyang. The rain continued, drumming softly on the roof of the car. Most of the city was asleep by this hour, and outside we saw not a single soul.

We rarely spoke. Chung sat in the front with his driver, a burly man with a grizzled face and small black eyes who never said a word and whose features were hardened into a permanent scowl. I sat in the back with old Kim Seung Il, who did nothing but gaze out the window, wrapped in his own thoughts.

Eventually we pulled into the underground garage of the Foreign Intelligence Building. There was nothing to distinguish this building from any others nearby; but in order to use the front entrance, one first had to walk through a small courtyard, which was monitored by surveillance cameras, and then pass two armed guards in the front lobby.

Tonight, however, I was introduced to a stairway that led up from the garage. Even at this hour the place was full of workers; intelligence is a twenty-four-hour-a-day operation. Chung led us to an elevator, and we stepped inside. He pressed button number 6 and settled back as the elevator crawled upward. "You're about to meet a very important man," he said, watching as the electronic indicator on the wall denoted the current floor. "Mr. Kim has met him several times, but this will be your first. I trust you'll make a good impression."

"Yes sir," I replied, now feverishly curious to know what this new assignment would be.

We reached the sixth floor and stepped out. Chung led us down a featureless white hall to an office at its far end, where a guard was seated behind a desk. Behind the desk was a closed door. As we entered, the guard stood, and Chung flashed an ID card. The guard nodded and opened the door, motioning us through.

Inside was a spacious office with a large desk at one end and a coffee table at the other. There were no windows, and the room was bathed in an eerie fluorescent light, like a laboratory. We were met by a tall, middle-aged man who moved with a feline grace, and I had the feeling that he must have spent years in the field.

"Ok Hwa, Seung Il," said Mr. Chung, "this is the Director. You're here at his wish."

I bowed to the Director. He exchanged a few words with Seung Il, whom he seemed to know well, and then motioned us to sit around the coffee table. Agent Chung, however, moved toward the door. "Good luck, comrades," he said. "This is top secret, and I'm not one who needs to know about it. So good luck." He exited.

We seated ourselves around the table. The Director, moving slowly and deliberately, withdrew a pack of cigarettes from his breast pocket and offered one to Seung Il, who accepted. He then offered one to me, but I declined. I had never been a smoker; and besides, I was so nervous that I just wanted to sit on my hands and get this meeting over with.

The Director lit his cigarette and that of Seung Il, and leaned back in his chair. "Comrades," he said. "I will start with the conclusion first. Your mission will be to destroy a South Korean airplane." He paused, allowing the words to sink in. I felt butterflies in my stomach and stared at him.

"The order, you may be interested to know, was written by Our Dear Leader himself, Kim Jung Il. *Handwritten*, that is." Again he paused, to make certain that we understood the weight of this information. I was now on the edge of my seat. That Kim Jung Il had written the order himself indicated that this would be a mission of truly paramount importance.

"This whole mission is in fact Our Dear Leader's own idea," continued the Director. "If I may say so, it's probably the most important undertaking that Foreign Intelligence has ever attempted. Our entire national destiny will depend on it.

"So—you must destroy a South Korean plane. That country, as you know, has been in considerable turmoil recently. The political climate is more volatile than at any time since the War of Liberation. Their constitution is being revised, and there are elections to be held toward the end of this year. By destroying this plane we intend to increase this sense of chaos and ultimately to prevent the Olympic Games from taking place in Seoul. Other nations will not want to risk their athletes, for fear that either their planes will be destroyed or that once in Seoul their athletes will not be safe from terrorist attacks.

"But that is just the beginning. If we succeed in preventing the Games from taking place, and if we succeed in worsening the political turmoil, there may well be the chance that our two Koreas could then be reunited. And that, as you know, is the great goal of our generation. If you comrades succeed in this mission, you will be nothing less than national heroes."

I could hardly believe my ears. I felt a mixture of awe and dread. I was flabbergasted that I would be entrusted with such a mission. And I must admit that not for a moment did I think of the moral issues involved, of the consequences of killing perhaps hundreds of people, either personally or in any larger ethical sense. This act of sabotage was a purely technical operation, a mere stepping-stone toward the great goal of Korean reunification. Considering the training I'd received throughout my life, how could I have believed otherwise? But now I keep asking myself if we are any less responsible for our actions even when we do them so unwittingly.

"There's no need to go into details at the moment," the Director went on, "but I can give you a broad outline of the plan. From Pyongyang you'll travel to Moscow and then Budapest and Vienna, where you'll spend several days acting again as a Japanese father and daughter on vacation. You'll then proceed to Belgrade, where again you'll pretend to be tourists. In this way your passports, having so many cities stamped on them, will also support your disguise.

"From Belgrade, you'll go to Baghdad, where the airplane will originate. You'll be met in the airport by two field agents, who will provide you with the explosives to destroy the plane. Before takeoff from Baghdad you'll plant the bomb in the overhead compartment and set the timer to detonate nine hours later. The plane is scheduled to continue to Abu Dhabi, Bangkok, and ultimately Seoul. You will disembark at Abu Dhabi, leaving the bomb aboard, and transfer to a flight bound for Rome via Amman. Once in Rome you'll proceed back to Vienna, where you'll remain in the Korean embassy for a few days before returning to Pyongyang."

I took a deep breath and looked at Kim Seung Il, who was watching me in turn. I thought I saw in his eyes the knowledge that comes only from the experience of many missions and the wisdom that comes only with age. I felt a little bit better knowing that he would be my partner. At the moment it seemed as though we two could accomplish anything.

"One more thing," said the Director. "Because of the extreme secrecy and importance of this mission, it will be the last one for each of you. After this it wouldn't be safe for you to continue working in the field, and what's more, you'll have performed the highest possible service for your country. As heroes, you will then retire with every luxury the Party can provide. And you, Ok Hwa, can return to your family." He paused and gave me a strange look that I couldn't read. "That's what you want, isn't it?"

I held his gaze. I wanted to jump out of my chair, more excited than ever, though I was a bit unsettled by his perceptivity. This mission would now be not only the greatest hope for my country but also the greatest hope for me personally. At that moment I felt strong enough to do anything. I felt an indescribable sense of pride and honor that I had been chosen by Our Dear Leader for such a mission; and though I had only the vaguest notion of precisely how the mission would actually lead to Korean reunification—to this day I have a hard time understanding politics—I just took what he said at face value. In a single stroke I would both serve my country and restore my family. "Have faith in us, Mr. Director." I spoke firmly, my eyes locked on his. "We will not fail."

CHAPTER NINE

AT THE TIME the days that followed seemed to crawl along at a snail's pace, though in retrospect they now seem like a blur. I was restless and anxious and had difficulty concentrating on anything. On the plane to Moscow I studied the mission plans over and over, for lack of anything better to do. By the time we landed, I knew every step of our long itinerary by heart:

- **Objective:** Destruction of Korean Air Flight 858 leaving Baghdad on November 29, bound for Seoul via Abu Dhabi and Bangkok.
- **Operation Team:** Leader, Special Agent Kim Seung Il; Assistant, Agent Kim Ok Hwa
- **Support Team:** Leader, Special Agent Choi Jung Soo; Assistant, Agent Choi Hong-Nark
- **Combat Specifics:** Depart Soonan Airport, Pyongyang on 11/12/87, 0830 hours, for Moscow. At Moscow stay at the North Korean embassy for two nights and obtain Aeroflot plane tickets departing Moscow to Budapest on 11/15, 0900 hours.
- **11/15:** Depart Moscow for Budapest, arriving at 1104

87

hours. Remain in Budapest for four nights at a Foreign Intelligence safehouse and then proceed to Vienna, entering Austria without passports with the aid of local operatives. In Vienna the Operation Team will stay at the Ampak Hotel and will be contacted under the code word *Nakayama*. While in Vienna the Operation Team is to use Japanese passports for any confirmation of identity and will purchase two sets of tickets:

1. The first tickets will be for Vienna–Belgrade–Baghdad–Abu Dhabi–Bangkok–Seoul.
2. The second tickets will be for Vienna–Belgrade–Baghdad–Abu Dhabi–Bahrain. These tickets will only be used in an emergency, as decoys.

Return tickets to Rome via Amman will be purchased separately in Abu Dhabi. After the first two sets of tickets have been purchased, the Operation Team will telephone Special Agent Choi in Baghdad. Operation Team will spend the rest of the time in Vienna pretending to be Japanese tourists.

- **11/24:** Leave Vienna at 1100 hours and arrive in Belgrade at 1400 hours, staying for four nights at the Metropolitan Hotel. Operation Team will again assume the guise of tourists.
- **11/28:** Leave Belgrade at 1430 and arrive at Baghdad at 2030 hours. Operation Team will wait for Korean Air Flight 858. During that time the Operation Team will meet the Support Team and receive the explosives to destroy the plane. After this meeting the bomb will be set to detonate in nine hours' time, but this may be changed in accordance with circumstance. The setting of the bomb should be done by Kim Seung Il; but if he is for any reason unable to do so, the job will fall to Kim Ok Hwa.

At 2345 hours, after boarding Flight 858, place the bomb in the overhead compartment. The Operation Team will then disembark at Abu Dhabi, leaving the explosives on the plane. If the bomb is discovered prior to deplaning, the Operation Team should maintain that it is not theirs.

- **11/29:** At 02:50 hours, after arriving in Abu Dhabi, proceed to board the next flight for Amman and Rome. Once in Rome, check into a hotel for a few days and resume the guise of Japanese sightseers.
- **12/1:** Leave Rome for Vienna and remain secluded in the North Korean embassy for several days before returning to Pyongyang under the guidance of local personnel.

When I had thoroughly memorized the itinerary, I pored over the instructions for setting the bomb:

Explosive Instructions for Panasonic Radio Model No. RF-082

- Setting the bomb to explode after nine hours:

  1. Flip the four switches at the bottom of the digital clock located on the right side of the radio-bomb.
  2. Move the alarm switch to the center of the word *Radio* so that it will explode nine hours after setting it.

- Setting the bomb to explode at any other time:

  1. Follow Step 1 as indicated above.
  2. Set the time to current time by pushing the three buttons under the digital clock.
  3. Press the Display button located on the right side of the digital clock.
  4. Set the desired time of explosion by pushing the three buttons at the right side of the digital clock.
  5. Follow Step 2 as indicated above.

Also on the flight was another agent from Foreign Intelligence, who at one point called Seung Il and me to the front of the cabin to discuss the mission in more detail. Because we were on a private flight, the airplane was almost empty, and there was a well-appointed lounge just behind the cockpit with a bar and video-playback system.

The agent's name was Cheon, a short and overweight man in his fifties with thinning gray hair and a rather comic facial tic, which gave him the appearance of continually smiling. We spent a few minutes reviewing the itinerary, which I had just been reading. But then he brought up a disturbing aspect of the mission that had never before been mentioned to us.

"The government has every confidence in you two," said Cheon. "Nevertheless the possibility of failure, however remote, cannot be ignored." He produced a pair of Marlboro cigarette packs and handed one to Seung Il and one to myself. "You'll notice that one cigarette in each pack is slightly marked in black ink. Those cigarettes contain ampules of liquid hydrocyanic acid located in the filter. If bitten, the ampules will release the cyanide, which will gassify and be absorbed into your bloodstreams. Death is virtually instantaneous." He looked at us in turn, and his facial tic made the whole matter seem like some joke. "If either of you are caught, you must take the poison before you can be interrogated. In the end the secrecy of this mission must be preserved at all costs. Do you understand this?"

I felt a sudden pang of nausea as I looked at the marked cigarette and the instant death it contained. Kim Seung Il nodded at Agent Cheon, who blandly resumed the briefing.

"I'm giving you comrades ten thousand American dollars for expenses. Spend it wisely. I'm leaving you in charge, Ok Hwa, of managing the financial aspects of the mission. Keep the money in a safe place and change it to other currencies as necessary." He reached into a briefcase that had been open on the table and extracted a thick packet of hundred-dollar bills. I gingerly took the packet and placed it in my purse.

"Lastly," said Cheon, "I want Ok Hwa to make certain that Kim Seung Il takes his medicine." He gave a genuine smile as he looked at the old warrior. "I know how you hate the taste of it, Seung Il, and I don't altogether trust you to take it yourself. And we need you healthy."

Kim shrugged, unamused. He turned to me and said, "Ok Hwa, could you leave us for a minute?"

"Of course," I replied. I stood and returned to my seat. I began to hear snatches of argument from the lounge. Seung Il, from what little I could overhear, seemed to be upset about the itinerary.

"Bullshit!" I heard him shout. "We're going to be in the middle of a bloody war zone! Iran and Iraq are still at war, and it's going to be impossible to smuggle explosives through the Baghdad airport. If something goes wrong, it's not just Ok Hwa and myself who will be in trouble. Our whole nation will look ridiculous. Don't you understand?"

"Look," snapped Cheon, "I have my orders. If you have a problem with them, I suggest you contact the Director."

"Fools," said Kim, almost inaudibly. "I mentioned this back at headquarters. You've all got your heads up your asses on this one." A moment later he strode into the cabin. He'd undergone stomach surgery before our departure; it was rumored that he was suffering from cancer. His face had a pale, unhealthy look, and he seemed a bit unsteady as he walked. He walked to the rear of the plane and went into the bathroom, slamming the door.

Cheon appeared then, walking over to my seat. He sat down next to me and said softly, "Your top priority during this mission is to look after his health. And if something happens to him, you will have to take over yourself."

"He looks ready to collapse already," I replied, my voice barely above a whisper.

"Part of it's the medication," he explained. "Comrade Kim may yet live many more years, but the stress of the mission is already starting to wear on him. This will only make his physical condition worse. Look after him, Ok Hwa. He's going to need you."

I nodded. "Don't worry. I'll manage." But I spoke with a lot more confidence than I felt.

He measured me for a moment, his face twitching away, before standing and walking back to the lounge. Kim appeared a few minutes later looking even more pallid than usual and sank into a chair across the aisle. "Fucking idiots," he muttered, reclining his seat and shutting his eyes.

I tried to sleep, but for the rest of the flight I couldn't. I found myself thinking back to Pyongyang, before our departure, when Kim and I had taken the Oath of Loyalty as the formal commencement of our mission:

> The entire nation is filled with the high spirit of socialism. The socialist revolution in South Korea is imminent, and our enemies have reached their most desperate hours. As we embark upon our mission, we vow the following:
>
> While we are undertaking the mission, we shall never forget the trust that the Party has placed in us and its concern on our behalves. We pledge that we will follow the Revolutionary Rules and that we will fully cooperate with each other to accomplish our mission.
>
> We shall preserve the integrity of Our Dear Leader with our lives.

Kim and I had been required both to speak these words and to sign a document containing them.

Opening my eyes, I looked over at him. He seemed to have fallen asleep and was breathing rather stertorously through his mouth. I felt a rush of affection for him and had an impetuous urge to touch his cheek.

Kim Seung Il was the father of seven children. His youngest daughter was married and over thirty. He had retired from Foreign Intelligence in 1984, but had earlier this year been asked to return. He had suffered from gallstones for many years, but during our first trip in 1984 he'd seemed in reasonably good health. Over the past few days I'd heard him reminisce about how he'd loved to spend his mornings during his former retirement fishing in a reservoir near his house. I knew that he would be as glad as I to get this whole thing over with.

I thought back to my abrupt departure from the camp. I'd packed quickly, and there was no time for long good-byes. I'd wished Sook Hee well, expecting to see her again, and then went to say farewell to Wul Chi. She'd come out into the living room and had first wrapped old Seung Il in a smothering embrace. "Come back in one piece, you hear?" she said, her eyes brimming with tears. Turning to me, she looked at me for a long moment before saying, "Have a good life, Ok Hwa. I will miss you."

I was a bit alarmed by this statement. "Wul Chi, I'm not leaving forever!"

She led me back to the kitchen, telling the men to wait. When we were alone, she embraced me and said, "Ok Hwa, I suppose it wouldn't be so difficult if you weren't so beautiful. But your combination of looks and brains was too good for them to resist. I hope someday they let you settle down and get married." She released me and looked into my eyes. "We won't see each other again. Good luck."

My own eyes were now filling with tears, and I could only nod dumbly at her before leaving. I knew if I stayed a moment longer, I'd lose my composure completely.

Coming back to the present, I let out a long sigh. I had known so many wonderful people over the years. I felt that this gave me all the more impetus to accomplish my mission, as though I would then be satisfying all their expectations of me. It seemed as though my whole life, from birth until this moment, hinged entirely on this mission.

The next few days passed with agonizing slowness. We refueled, deep in the Soviet Union, in the middle of the night. The ground was covered with snow, and the few lights that winked at us from the town seemed only to add to the desolation of the place. We then proceeded to Moscow, where we stayed only one harried day before leaving for Budapest.

Budapest, like Moscow, was already feeling the oncoming winter. We arrived late at night and discovered that no one at our embassy there had been informed of our arrival. Apparently our mission was so top-secret that only a very few people knew anything about it. Kim telephoned the embassy and, using a special code word, was transferred to a field agent. Half an hour later a chauffeur arrived from the embassy and was supposed to drive us to the safehouse where we'd spend the next few days, or at least he tried. After a while the man confessed that he was new to his job and didn't know Budapest very well. There was a light snowfall, and we wandered through the deserted streets for hours before locating the safehouse. By then it was three in the morning, and Kim and I fell asleep immediately.

Those few days in Budapest were unbearably dull. Kim Seung Il was too weak and worn out to go anywhere; and since we were not yet in our disguises as tourists, there was nothing interesting to do. I wandered around the neighborhood occasionally, to get a feel for this new city, but the weather was terrible, and I couldn't help feeling depressed. The television provided no consolation—I couldn't understand a word of what anyone was saying.

The agent who was in charge of looking after the safehouse was a middle-aged man named Chun. He had a beautiful wife, and she was always cooking exotic Western dinners for us. I spent much of the time chatting with her, though it was impossible, given our mutual constraints of secrecy, to say anything beyond the superficial.

The overriding problem we had to deal with was how we would enter Austria without visas. We needed to do so to avoid being traced; but thus far no one had explained to us how we would accomplish this. Since our superiors in Pyongyang had failed to produce an acceptable game plan, it fell to Special Agent Chun to come up with a solution.

The day before our scheduled departure he left the house early, claiming that he needed to do some reconnaissance. Kim, who was feeling better, suggested that we do some sightseeing, and Chun's wife, Liau, accompanied us. Kim insisted upon stopping at every coffeehouse we passed, telling us that he was thirsty. Exasperated, I told him that he should have brought a water bottle and that no one with his stomach problems should be drinking coffee at all! "Shut up," he replied peevishly. "I've lived long enough. I'll drink whatever the hell I want before I die."

Kim grew tired before long, and we were forced to return to the safehouse. Chun had returned, and told us triumphantly that he'd figured out a way to get us into Austria. "But let's worry about that tomorrow," he said. "Tonight we shall have a Western dinner at the Hilton Hotel."

On our way to dinner I had a chance to see more of Budapest. Although Hungary had for years been a communist country, there had recently, as a result of *perestroika*, been a conversion toward a more capitalist economy. Food, clothing, and luxury items were far more abundant than in North Korea, and perhaps the most breathtaking moment of all happened when we visited a flea market. I was literally awestruck by the variety of goods being sold, and handled one item after another for the sheer pleasure of *touching* them. Kim sensed my feelings and bought me a dress, and I wished at once that I could send a couple to my mother and Hyun Ok. Liau must have read my mind, for she offered to buy another dress and send the two back to Pyongyang. I gave her a big hug and longed for the day when North Korea would enjoy such a standard of living.

Our dinner that night was superb, of a quality never enjoyed by even the higher-ranking North Koreans, and I began to enjoy myself as I had on my first trip to Europe.

The following day was cold and rainy. Chun explained that he himself would drive us across the Austrian border, in his car with diplomatic plates, and that he would use his diplomatic passport. In this way there was an excellent chance that we would be allowed in without trouble.

We drove through the farm country that led to the border, and at the Hungarian security checkpoint we stopped. Chun handed the guard our three passports, with his own on top, and the guard waved us through. A short time later we came to the Austrian checkpoint, and moments later we were admitted into Austria proper.

I felt a huge sense of relief after that. Chun handed us our Japanese passports, which we would be using from now on. As we drove, I was impressed by the Western-style houses, which were larger and seemed sturdier than their Korean counterparts. The scenery was beautiful, and I remembered from my earlier trip the majesty of the Alps.

Once in Vienna, we stopped at a tourist bureau, and Kim went inside to confirm our booking at the Ampak Hotel. He was gone more than half an hour, and Chun and I began to worry. Had he collapsed? Had he been arrested? Chun was about to go inside when Kim wandered out, with no sense of urgency, and got into the car. He didn't even mention his long absence and ordered Chun rather curtly to proceed to the hotel.

By the time we checked in, Seung Il could barely stand up.

As soon as we entered our room, he threw himself on the bed and was asleep within seconds. I unpacked my luggage and flicked idly through a magazine that I'd brought from Pyongyang. Kim slept for about an hour, and when he woke, it was time to collect our tickets.

This was the most crucial aspect of our stay in Vienna. The airline tickets had been purchased ahead of time by someone in Foreign Intelligence, and we were due to meet a field agent later in the day. We proceeded outside into a light drizzle and opened our umbrellas. After walking a short distance we found a pay phone, and Kim fumbled in his pockets for his phone list. Chun, before leaving, had left us each a coded list of secure telephone numbers throughout Europe, which would put us in touch with Foreign Intelligence personnel in various locations. Kim dialed the special line into the North Korean embassy in Vienna and spoke briefly before hanging up.

"Half an hour," he said as we stepped out of the phone booth. He pointed to a park just across the street. "There's a stream that runs through the middle of that park. We're to meet the field agent on the park bench nearest to the bridge."

We crossed the street and wandered into the park's interior. The leaves had long fallen from the trees, and there were few people about. We soon came upon the stream and followed its course until we came across a small stone bridge that spanned the water. There was a park bench nearby, and we seated ourselves to wait in the damp cold.

Twenty minutes later a well-dressed woman with a wide-brimmed hat came toward us from the other side of the stream. She crossed the bridge, and as she drew closer, I saw that she looked Korean. She walked by us without stopping, but I heard her say the word *Nakayama* as she passed. Seung Il repeated the word, not looking at her. I watched her retreat, noticing her drop something in a nearby trash can. Soon she was out of sight.

Kim waited a few minutes more and then told me that we could leave. We walked down the same path as the woman, and as we reached the trash can, Kim looked around quickly before reaching inside and extracting a large brown envelope. As we walked on, he opened the envelope and peered inside.

"Excellent," he said. "We may pull this thing off after all."

We spent the next few days touring Vienna. Everywhere we went, we took pictures, acting the perfect tourists. This was not merely for the sake of appearances; our superiors in Pyongyang would be interested in our photographs, for they would prove that we were following our instructions to the letter and not spending all our time in fancy stores, lured by capitalist decadence!

One afternoon we had lunch in a Chinese restaurant, and I was glad for a reprieve from Western food. It was not that I disliked it, but I had had nothing else for the past week and I was glad to have something more familiar.

During lunch Kim abruptly clutched his stomach and nearly fell out of his chair. "Mayumi," he said—for we were not allowed to use our Korean names during the mission—"I can't walk."

I went around the table to help him. "You've got to, Shinichi. We can't exactly call an ambulance."

I assisted him to his feet. After settling the bill I helped him back to the hotel. I was supporting nearly his whole weight, and his breath was coming in quick gasps. I worried for a moment that he was about to die, but when we reached the hotel, he said he was better.

He walked through the lobby under his own power, reluctant to draw any attention to us. When we reached our room, he collapsed on the bed. I pulled out his medicine and forced him to take it. Soon he was asleep. I felt like fainting, I was so relieved.

I spent the afternoon watching Austrian television and dozed off myself. Seung Il woke toward evening, and we were able to go out for a light meal. When we returned, we spent some time working with a dummy bomb unit to practice for the real thing.

We spent our last day in Vienna shopping. As usual we would be expected to buy gifts for high government officials, to be presented upon our return. Kim and I each had two hundred dollars spending money for ourselves, and we soon learned that that could not buy very much in Vienna! We browsed through shop after shop, and compared with the well-dressed European women in their mink coats, we felt inadequate as supposedly rich Japanese tourists, especially because the real Japanese tourists truly were as wealthy as the Europeans. Most of the clothes were too big for me, and we ended up buying rather meaningless little items, such as a battery for Seung Il's watch and five pairs of stockings for me.

I was not sad to leave Vienna. It is a beautiful city, but once we'd picked up the airline tickets, I felt as though we had no real purpose there. We were merely passing time, and coming as we did from a socialist country, it was fascinating but still quite foreign to spend so much time in Western Europe.

Belgrade promised to be different. Yugoslavia, though alienated from the other Soviet Bloc countries, was a socialist country and was rumored to be more prosperous than North Korea. (Then again, everywhere I'd been was better off than North Korea.) I was a bit worried about using Japanese passports in a socialist nation; I thought that they'd probably watch us more closely. Some researcher at Foreign Intelligence in Pyongyang had confirmed that Belgrade *does* attract Japanese tourists, but only in small numbers. Even our superiors had admitted that it might be difficult.

My fear grew when I discovered that we were the only Japanese passengers on the flight to Belgrade. In Vienna we had avoided contact with Asians; now we felt conspicuous. I mentioned this to Kim Seung Il, who replied—not for the first or last time—that our itinerary had been flawed from the start.

We entered Belgrade without a hitch, however, and in the airport terminal found dozens of cab drivers vying for our patronage. As we proceeded to the Hotel Intercontinental, where we would be staying, my first impression of Belgrade was that it was dirtier, drearier, and far more depressing than Vienna. The weather was bleak, the city rather chaotic, and neither the scenery nor the architecture was of particular interest to me.

Our stay was even duller than in Vienna. Kim felt ill most of the time, but managed to stagger outside each day for a few hours. One day we went into a department store, and Kim spent the better part of an hour trying on hats. I walked into the lingerie section, amazed at the variety and frilly, romantic, and sexually charged quality of the merchandise. I was twenty-five years old, a virgin, and had no prospects to marry anytime soon—if ever.

Sex as a whole formed a curious dilemma for me. Neither I nor any woman I'd grown up with was ignorant of sexual chemistry between men and women, yet from childhood we were taught that sex was forbidden outside marriage. Even throughout college, men and women were separated. Once a couple was married, sex was permitted only for procreation, since our socialism had little use for concepts such as romance. North Korea was a distinctly unsensual society, and part of my outlook reflected that. How ironic, therefore, that our superiors expected us women field agents to be able to seduce men and manipulate them as a mission might require. But despite my education, I was well aware of the erotic possibilities between the sexes, and I occasionally felt a sense of longing and acute loneliness.

I bought some lacy underwear, which would never have been available in North Korea, and then searched for Kim Seung Il. He was nowhere to be seen. As I wandered through the aisles, I was accosted by a bedraggled old schizophrenic, who began yelling obscenities (or so they seemed) at me and even trying to strike me with his umbrella. I immediately became terrified at the attention this would draw, and unconsciously my training took over. I slipped inside his guard, grabbed his umbrella hand, and drove my knee into his groin. At the same time I twisted his arm around and flipped him onto the carpeted floor. I knelt beside him, my hand poised to strike his face, but he was doubled up, clutching his groin, and there was no need for me to do so. Fortunately we were concealed by the racks of underwear that surrounded us, and no one seemed to have noticed. I snatched up my bags and fled the store, wondering desperately where the hell Kim was.

Anything could have happened to him, I thought, as I half ran back to the hotel. Heart attack, arrest—he might even have deserted me! I was angry and nervous, and the prospect of continuing the mission alone was absolutely terrifying.

Back at the hotel I returned to our room and found Kim inside, unwrapping some food parcels on the table. I was enormously relieved to see him, and then my joy turned quickly into anger. "Where the hell were you?" I shouted, throwing my bags onto my bed and confronting him. "I looked everywhere for you! Why the hell did you leave me there alone?"

He seemed amused at my fury, and by way of reply pointed to the table. "I was buying some sausage and bread. I suggest we eat it while it's fresh, eh?"

I stood there fuming. I was shocked that he had left me and shocked that he seemed oblivious to my anger. He smiled and raised his hands to placate me.

"Mayumi, I was looking for you as well. Once I'd finished with the hats, I couldn't find you anywhere. I trusted that you'd have the sense to return to the hotel, which is exactly what I did myself. On the way I came across this sausage, which as we speak is getting cold." He offered a slice of bread to me, which I grabbed out of his hand and shoved into my mouth. He continued to stare at me, amused, and after a moment I burst out laughing. I aimed a playful side kick at his face, and despite his age he leaped back immediately, assuming a combat stance. "You idiot," I mumbled at him, still laughing as I chewed the bread. "I was worried about you."

We spent the rest of the time in Belgrade preparing for the trip to Baghdad. Kim and I practiced arming the dummy bomb again and again, and by the time we were ready to leave, I could have done it in my sleep. On the day of departure we carefully packed our suitcases and checked the room twice to make sure that we weren't leaving anything behind that could be used to trace us.

"This is it, Mayumi," said Seung Il as we shut the door and walked toward the elevator. "Combat time."

CHAPTER TEN

THERE IT STOOD on the runway, not a hundred yards away: Korean Air Flight 858. I stared at it through the huge window of the airport terminal, watching as the ground crew completed their maintenance work. If only they could know what would happen today. . . .

It was November 28, just before sunset. Even so late in the year Baghdad was stiflingly hot. We had just arrived from Belgrade as scheduled and in a few hours would take off for Abu Dhabi. Today, at last, after all the preparation, the action would begin.

Kim Seung Il stood beside me, and I sensed that he shared my thoughts. He reached out and squeezed my hand for a moment in a rare display of affection. It suited our roles well—a father's loving gesture to his daughter. Despite his many years, despite his experience, I knew that he was as nervous as I. For a moment I thought about how he really had become a father figure during this mission. And then I thought of my own family, and I longed to go home to them.

"Soon, Ok Hwa," he whispered, daring to use my Korean name for the first time. "Soon."

As we turned from the window, we spotted two well-dressed Koreans walking toward us through the crowd. One held a large briefcase. I knew immediately that these were our contacts and that the briefcase contained the bomb. I pretended I was calm, but my stomach was in knots.

The field agents were both named Choi, and indeed they bore an eerie resemblance to each other, though they were supposedly unrelated. They were exactly the same height and wore expensive black suits and fashionable wire-rimmed sunglasses. Their hair was slicked back in the same style, and for a moment I thought I was looking at twins.

The older of the two men held the rank of field director; the younger held the rank of special agent. After we exchanged greetings and pleasantries, we accompanied the Chois to the airport bar for a drink. With seemingly genuine concern, Director Choi asked about Mr. Kim's health, which had not improved since we left Pyongyang.

"This will be my last mission," replied Kim.

Director Choi patted him on the shoulder. "If that is so, then I can think of no better assignment to complete your distinguished career." He sipped his drink and then asked, "I trust that you both remember how to set the timer?"

"Of course," replied Kim.

"Excellent." He finished his drink and glanced at his watch. "Well, I think we should be going. It wouldn't be wise for us to be seen with you." He looked at Kim and me in turn. "Good luck to both of you."

We shook hands and they left, leaving the briefcase with us. I felt relieved, somehow, that Kim would be carrying it and not I.

"Remember," Kim said to me as we walked toward the gate. "The liquid explosives in the bottle will increase the explosive power of the radio bomb, so they must be kept together at all times." He glanced around the terminal to make sure no one could hear us. "Also," he continued, speaking even more softly, "remember that the batteries in the radio cannot be replaced by other batteries, so you must not lose them." He gave a rare smile and said in a wry voice, "And be sure not to confuse my medicine with the liquid explosive either."

We separated at the security checkpoint. In this part of the world they check not only your luggage but your bodies as well. Outwardly I remained calm, but inside, my pulse was racing, and I even felt a bit light-headed.

Everything proceeded smoothly until the special agent—a dour, unsmiling woman in her thirties—discovered the batteries in the briefcase, along with what appeared to be a bottle of water. At once she plucked them out and said, "No batteries can be brought aboard a plane at this airport."

At once I panicked. Without the batteries the bomb would fail to detonate and our long, intricately planned, and costly mission would be useless, our efforts worth nothing. I begged her, almost crying, to return the batteries. She remained adamant and began to grow suspicious why anyone should care so much about a few simple batteries. She tossed them in the garbage can, and I could see she was becoming impatient.

As I drew fresh breath to argue more, knowing it was unthinkable for me to return to North Korea as a failure, I spotted Mr. Kim walking toward me, his own inspection complete. At that moment he seemed like a savior, and I quickly told him what had happened. He frowned and looked inside the garbage can and a moment later reached in to extract the batteries. He inserted them into the radio and turned it on to verify that it worked.

"Look," he told the special agent. "These batteries are for this radio, nothing more. They have never caused any trouble in the other airports where we've traveled. If you refuse to allow us to carry them aboard, you can be assured that I will lodge a complaint with the Iraqi embassy in Tokyo immediately upon my return. Oh, and not to mention the Japanese embassy in Baghdad as well."

At that moment I began to understand the importance of Japanese economic power. The woman hesitated and glanced toward another special agent who had been watching nearby.

"Please accept my apologies," he said, stepping forward. "We are only following regulations, you must understand." He frowned for a moment and then said, "As you wish. You may bring them aboard."

I felt an enormous sense of relief. At last we were able to proceed. Then we came upon another checkpoint and had to submit to the same inspection all over again. This time, however, Mr. Kim hid the radio under his belt, and we passed through without incident.

"I told those idiots in Pyongyang that we'd have trouble here," Kim muttered as we walked on.

As we approached the gate, we saw a large number of South Koreans gathered in the lounge. We almost had the feeling that we were in a South Korean airport. We managed to find some seats apart from the others, and I sat down. Kim went to the rest room carrying the briefcase, but returned a minute later. "Mayumi, the men's rest room is full. You must take the bomb into the women's rest room and set it yourself."

I stared at him for a moment, feeling suddenly anxious. While I had been trained to set the bomb, I had assumed throughout our mission that everything would go according to plan, and that Mr. Kim would take care of this. I knew, as our eyes met, that he was measuring me. I managed to hold his gaze and say, "Of course. I'll be right back."

Inside the women's rest room I locked myself in a stall and took out the radio. I had practiced this dozens of times on an unloaded bomb; but now, with the real thing, I couldn't help feeling scared stiff. My hands were shaking, and no amount of willpower could steady them. At last I resolved that I just had to go ahead and do it. I glanced at my watch. It was 10:40 P.M. We would be boarding the plane in twenty minutes. Step by rehearsed step, as methodically as possible, I set the alarm timer to go off in nine hours' time. And then, holding my breath and half expecting the thing to explode then and there, I set the detonation switch to Active.

There. I had done it. I sighed with relief and paused for a moment, thinking that now there was no turning back. At that moment I felt no guilt or remorse at what I was doing; I thought only of completing the mission and not letting my country down.

But as I caught a glimpse of myself in the mirror on the way out, looking at the face lined with anxiety and fatigue stemming from the past few days, I could not help wondering for a moment how in the world I had gotten here. For a moment I saw the face I had known as a child and not the mature, adult face that stared at me now. It seemed strange at that moment, suddenly alien, as though I'd become an adult without realizing it and had forgotten who I was. I could see my mother's face in my own, and I wondered what she would have thought of me now. I had a strong feeling that she wouldn't approve, regardless of the honors I would receive, and it was a long moment before I could pull myself away.

As I rejoined Mr. Kim in the lounge, he raised his eyebrows at me inquiringly. I nodded, giving a faint smile, and sat next to him to await the boarding call.

Mr. Kim took out a bottle of pills and shook four into his hand. Two he gulped down himself and handed the other two to me. "For your nerves," he said, and gratefully I accepted.

A voice came over the loudspeaker; the boarding procedure was commencing. We got onto a bus that would take us out to the airplane. Though it was a short distance, it felt like miles. Night had fallen on Baghdad, and the plane towered over us, majestically lit in the darkness.

When I think now of the crowd in the courtroom at my sentencing, it is impossible not to think of that moment on the bus. The passengers were almost all South Korean, talking animatedly among themselves. At the time I felt a pang of sympathy. Though they were "South" Koreans, I felt as though these were my people. The divide between us seemed so artificial. I told myself that my mission was for the good of both our countries. That was what I'd been told, and I believed it.

But now, looking back, I can only see the tearstained faces of the families in the courtroom, and I try to relate those faces with the laughing faces on the bus. I wonder who was related to whom.

The bus stopped, interrupting my thoughts. We stepped down onto the pavement and walked the short distance to the flight of stairs that led up to the door. At the top a pair of stewardesses greeted us, and another one came forward to help us to our seats.

Mr. Kim placed our bags in the overhead compartment. I studied him as he did so, noting the exhaustion on his face. At that moment he looked old and feeble, but I couldn't help thinking that he possessed a certain majesty as well, this veteran spy who had seen so much in his seventy years.

I sat by the window, and Mr. Kim in the middle. The aisle seat was soon taken by a Caucasian woman. I was oddly relieved that she was not South Korean, but then wondered whether she would, within hours, be dead as well. It was an eerie feeling.

I had calmed down as we boarded, but now I began to be frightened again. Especially with the night outside, the cabin seemed like its own little world, very confining. I felt trapped, claustrophobic. Moreover there was always the possibility that the bomb would go off before it was supposed to. At any moment I might die and never know what had happened. It was not a pleasant thought.

The plane took off on schedule. I tried to sleep but could not, so instead I listened to the conversations around me. Most of the South Koreans seemed to be laborers of some sort, perhaps oil workers, and they were clearly glad to be going home. Some were complaining about their companies and their working conditions, and this reaffirmed that South Korean corporations exploited their workers, as we'd been taught.

Whenever the stewardesses walked by, my heartbeat would accelerate. There also seemed to be a security guard seated nearby, who was looking around at the other passengers. I had the feeling that he was always staring at me.

Again I tried to calm myself. I thought about the fact that if I succeeded, I would be awarded the highest honor my country could give. I also thought about something I'd been told back in Pyongyang, before the mission had started. I'd been told that I would never be used as an agent again, to protect the secrecy of the mission. This bolstered the hope that I could return to my family, which I wanted more than anything in the world.

The other passengers fell asleep, and the cabin lights were turned off, leaving the plane in darkness. There was only the constant hum of the engines. I glanced at Mr. Kim, who appeared to be in deep meditation. But I could see one of the veins in his neck throbbing with each heartbeat, and I noticed that his breathing was very quick.

That flight, though it lasted only an hour, seemed like an eternity. All the worries and difficulties prior to sitting in that plane had been nothing compared with the anxiety I felt now. There was nothing to do but just *wait*. When the pilot's voice came over the intercom announcing our approach to Abu Dhabi, I jumped in my seat. Mr. Kim and I looked at each other simultaneously, and I think we both had the same hint of desperation in our faces. The closer the plane came to landing, the more nervous I became, as if I was counting down to imminent disaster.

At last the plane touched down, but once it had slowed, it took some time before we reached the gate. We stood up at once and grabbed our luggage from the overhead compartment. I stared for a moment at the briefcase that contained the explosive, and it looked so innocuous. It was hard to believe that there was a bomb inside that could destroy this airplane. I shuddered, and then turned my back on it forever.

There was another long delay as we waited to disembark. The line crawled along; many of the passengers continuing to Seoul were disembarking just to stretch their legs. *Move, dammit!* I thought, clenching my teeth. *Move!!!*

It seemed like another eternity standing in the aisle before we reached the exit, and even then I half expected some invisible hand to yank me back inside, or to see some steward come up with our briefcase, asking if it was ours. But the stewardess at the door merely smiled and said, "Good-bye. Thank you for flying with us."

My legs shook as we disembarked, and I could barely walk straight. Still, I felt a huge sense of relief. I felt like I had been through a grueling ordeal and had at last come out the other side. I looked at Mr. Kim, and he smiled.

Our relief was short-lived. In the airport lounge a security guard was collecting tickets and passports from the transit passengers (that is, those who were switching flights) and handing out yellow boarding passes to those who were continuing on the same flight.

Immediately Kim looked flustered. According to our plan, we were supposed to transfer to Jordanian Airlines Flight 603, which would take us to Rome via Amman. But now a hitch developed—the guard was, altogether unexpectedly, asking us to turn in our tickets.

The problem was this: If we gave him the Abu Dhabi–Amman–Rome tickets, he would most likely become instantly suspicious. Why would a Japanese father and daughter fly to Abu Dhabi from Baghdad and then immediately proceed to Amman and Rome, when there would have been plenty of flights to Rome directly from Baghdad? Nor, moreover, could we claim to be staying in Abu Dhabi, which would have required that we obtain a visa—impossible, since Japan had no formal agreement with the United Arab Emirates.

We had never anticipated such a problem. No other airport in the world, at least to our knowledge, collected the passengers' tickets when they were merely passing through. Things were now becoming dangerous.

For this reason, when the guard reached us, we gave him our two backup tickets, showing Vienna–Baghdad–Bahrain. The guard disappeared with our tickets, saying that he would take care of the boarding procedures.

"What do we do now?" I whispered to Kim.

"We must leave Abu Dhabi as soon as possible," he replied. "We'll have to go to Bahrain first and fly to Rome from there."

Flight 858 took off for Bangkok and Seoul, and I watched as its light grew fainter and fainter in the night sky. I felt a vague mixture of anticipation and dread as I watched it vanish. I could not stop thinking about the South Koreans and the way they had been laughing.

Hours passed. It was the middle of the night in Abu Dhabi, and the airport was quiet. The guard who had taken our tickets was conversing with some colleagues at the far end of the waiting room and occasionally glancing in our direction. At one point Mr. Kim walked over to ask what had happened to our tickets. The guard replied that we would receive them before our plane left at nine o'clock and not to worry.

Mr. Kim sat down, rubbing his face with his hands, and complained bitterly that he'd known from the start that our itinerary had been flawed. Then, sensing that he might frighten me with such words, he tried to reassure me, saying, "A plane accident is never resolved quickly. We should be back in Pyongyang before they start looking for us." But he looked as if he didn't believe his own words, and I said nothing.

Toward dawn I looked at my watch. The bomb would be detonating at 6:00 A.M. our time; it was 5:54. I thought of the plane, which would by now be over the Andaman Sea near Burma. At any moment now . . .

I fell into a fitful sleep. When I woke, it was daylight, and soon our flight would be leaving. The guard at last returned our passports and tickets, and we boarded the flight to Bahrain. I gave a huge sigh of relief as we took off, feeling incredibly glad to be out of Abu Dhabi.

We arrived in Bahrain an hour later, on the morning of Sunday, November 29. We did not feel particularly safe there either and tried immediately to book a flight to Rome. Since our tickets originated in Abu Dhabi, however, it would be necessary to have them revalidated at the airline ticket office, which was closed on Sundays. Shaking his head in exasperation, Mr. Kim said that we'd have to stay overnight here in Bahrain, and we obtained three-day transit visas.

We booked a room by telephone at the Hotel Intercontinental and hired a taxi to get us there. Once we arrived there, we spent much of the day sleeping. There was nothing to do but wait.

On Monday morning we tried to book a flight to Rome, but were told that it was full and that we'd have to wait until Tuesday.

We spent Monday touring Manama, to make it look as if we were Japanese vacationers; but neither of us remembered a thing that we saw. We did some shopping to fill the time; Mr. Kim bought us some fruit and sandwiches for supper, and we brought them to our hotel room to eat.

As we were eating, the phone rang. I was so startled that I dropped the banana I'd been peeling. No one knew we were staying here, not even our superiors. There was no reason for anyone to call us here.

I looked at Mr. Kim, feeling the blood drain from my face. He returned my gaze for a moment before picking up the phone. "Yes?"

He listened for a moment and then hung up. He stood and walked to the window, his hands clasped behind his back. I asked him what was wrong, and he wouldn't answer. I could see from the set of his jaw that he was nervous. My heart began to race and my mouth went dry. A few moments later the phone rang again. He walked over and answered and then motioned me for the passports, which I gave to him. I heard him reading our names and passport numbers, and then he hung up.

"That was the Japanese embassy." He sighed, and looked at me before adding, "Don't worry. It won't be easy for them to trace us."

I held his gaze and replied, "I don't believe that." And I didn't. Suddenly I had the premonition that the authorities knew exactly who and where we were.

He shrugged, his face expressionless. I stood and began to clean up the table when the phone rang again. Mr. Kim answered, listened briefly, and hung up.

"Mayumi, there are two men from the Korean embassy in the lobby. They're coming up to see us now. Pretend to be asleep and let me handle this."

Now panicking, I climbed into the bed, forgetting to remove my shoes. I faced the wall and pulled the covers up to my neck. I wanted to sink into that bed until I disappeared. At that moment my awful premonition seemed confirmed, and I knew that there was no hope for us.

Moments later we heard a knock at the door. Kim opened the door and admitted the two men.

"Forgive me," said Kim, after introducing himself, "but my daughter is exhausted and must rest."

They all sat at the table. Because the Koreans did not speak Japanese, the conversation struggled along in halting English. The Koreans frequently swore in frustration, but Mr. Kim kept up his act.

At last they got their story out. They said that Korean Air Flight 858 to Seoul, carrying 115 passengers, had disappeared before reaching its transit stop in Bangkok and was believed to have crashed. I could tell from their tones that they suspected our involvement, and they asked what our next destination was.

For a moment I thought of the plane crashing. I confess that I felt no remorse at the time and that I was relieved to know for certain that we had accomplished our mission and been faithful to Kim Il Sung and Kim Jung Il. I was sure now that the 1988 Olympics would not take place in Seoul and that I had been part of an important step toward Korean reunification.

The Koreans left, promising to return the next day. A few hours later we heard another knock at the door, and Kim opened it slightly. A parcel of chocolate was thrust in at us, and then the deliverer withdrew. It was clear they were watching us.

I did not sleep that night. Mr. Kim, who was utterly exhausted, fell into a deep sleep and snored loudly the entire night. I could only stare at the ceiling and glance at the clock every few minutes. I felt numb. It was only a matter of time, I told myself, before they would arrest us.

Mr. Kim continued to sleep like a log, even after daybreak. I shook him awake impatiently, and we packed in a hurry to make the plane on time. When at last we were finished and I was walking to the door, he called me.

"Mayumi, wait."

I turned to him. His face was serious, and he could not hold my gaze for long. He reached into a pocket and handed me the Marlboro pack, which he'd been keeping. "Should worse come to worst," he said quietly, and I noticed that his hand was trembling as he gave it to me.

Both of us knew, I think, that we were done for. But neither of us expected actually to have to use the poison. Neither of us could be sure that we had such courage.

As we walked to the elevator, Mr. Kim repeated his words of two days ago: "I told those idiots about the itinerary. I told them. When we get back, I will raise hell!"

We checked out immediately, skipping breakfast. We stepped outside into the blinding morning light, ignoring the suspicious gazes of the hotel staff. Our fear had to be obvious to anyone who saw us. No matter how hard we tried, we could not act calmly.

We flagged a cab and raced to the airport. As the barren landscape flashed by, I clutched the cigarette pack, praying that I would not have to use it. It was strange to hold it like that, to know that the tiny amount of poison inside could kill me instantly. I felt sick to my stomach at the thought.

We arrived at the airport without incident, and Mr. Kim hastened to get our boarding passes. I scanned the concourse for signs of pursuit, but saw none. At length Kim rejoined me, and we sped to the gate. We lined up behind the other passengers to board, and I began to hope we might escape after all.

Then I heard a voice behind me speaking in fluent Japanese.

"May I see your passports, please?"

I turned and saw a tall Oriental man standing nearby. Wordlessly we handed him our passports, and he walked off and vanished.

Kim and I were directed to step out of line and had to stand by and watch as the other passengers boarded the plane. In the back of my mind I could hear the Director's voice back in Pyongyang saying, "You comrades must keep in mind the utmost secrecy of this mission. In the worst case, you must be prepared to bite the poisoned ampules to preserve this secret. Remember that when you forfeit your physical lives, your political lives will continue for all eternity."

And I thought, *Yes. I will be a proud daughter of the fatherland and gladly give my life for its reunification.*

For the first time in days I actually felt calm.

Then I heard the announcement that the plane bound for Rome was taking off. I turned to the window and watched the plane taxi away, taking with it my last hopes. My resolution of only moments before was shattered. It was foolish to pretend I was so strong.

As I turned away, I saw the Oriental man returning with our passports, his face grim. "You must remain where you are. Both of you."

"For what reason?" asked Mr. Kim.

"I am from the Japanese embassy in Bahrain. The passport belonging to Mayumi Hachiya has been determined to be a fake, and you will be held for questioning. The police will be arriving momentarily, and I warn you not to try anything foolish."

He wandered off a short distance, scanning the hallway, as if to make sure that we were alone.

Kim touched my shoulder, and I turned to him. His face was grave.

"Ok Hwa, you must be strong and bite the ampule. Now that we've been discovered, it would only prolong your agony if you don't. I have no regret to die now. I have lived long enough. But you"—his voice faltered, and it was a moment before he could look at me again—"I'm so sorry."

I knew that the old man was crying inside, and I was a bit shocked to see this human side of Kim Seung Il. For here right before me was one of North Korea's most accomplished secret agents, a true revolutionary fighter. Throughout our mission, despite his age, despite his illness, and despite the unfortunate twist our fates had taken, he had never given in to his fears. And now at last he was crumbling—not for himself but for me.

I could not speak as the tears streamed down my cheeks, but I nodded to communicate my resolve.

Then, in my mind's eye, I unexpectedly saw my mother's face.

The few times I had visited home during my training—no more than once every two or three years—she had always welcomed me back and had been happy to see me in such good health. Whenever I left, it would take all her effort to maintain her composure. She was so sad to see me go. At the time I rarely noticed her feelings. I would follow the escorting instructor back to the training camp, proud to have been chosen by the Party. I felt now that I had failed her, the woman who had worked so hard to raise me. I was ashamed at my vanity and saw too late the mistakes I had made. No Party was worth neglecting one's family for.

Forgive me, Mother. Please understand. . . .

I must die. For it would be she, and not just I, who would pay for my failures.

I looked at Mr. Kim, who was chain-smoking next to me. "Father, give me a signal when I should bite the ampule."

He was buried in his thoughts and nodded dispassionately. His face was blank as he exhaled. He was probably thinking about his own family.

At that moment four or five Bahraini police officers strode into the room and ordered us to go with them. We were separated, and I was taken to a small, featureless office to be searched.

The women who conducted the search were thorough. They examined every part of my body, as if not to miss a hair. They rummaged carefully through my makeup case. But they did not seem to pay much attention to the cigarettes, which I had put into my black shoulder bag.

When I returned to the hallway, Kim was waiting for me. A

Bahraini policeman stood nearby. Kim looked at me, eyebrows raised, as if to ask whether the cigarettes were safe. I smiled in reply, and he looked relieved. He handed me a Japanese cigarette to make it seem as though I smoked frequently, so that when the critical moment came, I would not look too suspicious.

That did it.

As I took the cigarette and pulled a lighter from my shoulder bag, one of the female officers who'd searched me asked for the bag. Unable to refuse, I took out the Marlboro pack and handed her the bag. She then motioned for the pack as well. I took out the poisoned cigarette and gave her the pack. No matter how suspicious it may have looked, I could not afford to give her that cigarette. Everything hinged on that ampule. I had to keep it in my hand.

The officer barked something incomprehensible at me and held out her hand. I glanced at Mr. Kim, who shook his head. For a moment I froze, and the officer grabbed the cigarette from my hand. Without thinking, I snatched it back. There was no time to hesitate. I bit down on the ampule before she could react. I saw her jumping toward me, shrieking, but I did not care. At that moment I was being drawn inexorably into a sweet, soothing darkness.

The faithful daughter of Kim Il Sung, trained for years like some obedient dog, died at that moment.

It was all over; I was freed from all pain. The pitch blackness enveloped me like a comforting blanket. *Everything was over. . . .*

CHAPTER ELEVEN

IN THE CENTER of a white room I found myself laid still.

Voices nearby, speaking Bahraini and English, drifted into my consciousness. The room was windowless; it could have been day or night. My left hand was cuffed to the bed. An oxygen tube had been placed in my nostrils, and another tube ran down my throat, presumably to clean out my stomach. An IV ran out of my right arm.

I could not think clearly. My senses were clouded from either anesthesia or sheer exhaustion. It took tremendous effort to keep my eyes open. I remember thinking that it was all a dream and that this white room was some way station between one world and the next. Vaguely I recalled the fact that I had taken poison, and my first thought was that it had worked.

I lay there for some time in dazed limbo, thinking of absolutely nothing. I swam between consciousness and sleep, my perceptions dull and unfocused. Bit by bit, however, I regained a semblance of clarity and turned my head to see two nurses in traditional Arab clothes sitting by the bed watching me. Near the doorway stood two swarthy men in combat fatigues, machine guns cocked at 45-degree angles: ready-to-fire position. Alarmed, my first reaction was to pinch my thigh.

Nothing happened. This was not a dream.

No! I thought. *I am alive.*

I groaned in despair. Why wasn't I dead? I must not have inhaled enough of the poison. I had come close to death, that much seemed obvious, but I had evidently not come close enough.

I was not happy to be alive. I knew right away that the agony had just begun.

My weakened condition and my newfound panic induced a sort of delirium upon me. I noticed that one of the nurses had a pair of scissors in one of her pockets. I strained to reach them, hoping to impale myself before they could stop me, but I was securely chained to the bed and I could not move.

At length the tubes were removed from my nose and mouth, and I immediately bit my tongue as hard as I could. I had heard stories during my childhood that one could kill oneself by doing so. I succeeded only in causing myself excruciating pain. It seems absurd in retrospect, of course, that I actually believed those old wives' tales.

Next I tried to suffocate myself. I held my breath until my cheeks puffed up, pushing myself as far as I could. *A little longer,* I thought, *a little longer.* But at the last moment I was unable to keep it up and found myself panting for breath. I didn't realize at the time that the moment I lost consciousness, my body would take over, and I would start breathing again anyway.

Damn it! my thoughts raged. *Why can't I fucking kill myself?!*

I wondered then if Kim Seung Il had also survived. Probably not; if the cyanide hadn't killed him (assuming he had taken it), then the sheer stress of our capture would have been enough to finish him off. It seemed amazing that he had survived as long as he had.

Thinking about him frightened me. I missed him, and I was now truly, utterly alone.

I must be strong, I thought. *The Dear Leader himself has put his faith in me. I will die for my country, die for reunification. I cannot let my country down.*

At least one thing was certain: The plane had been destroyed.

At that moment I no longer felt proud of my mission. Before our capture, as I have said, I thought primarily about fulfilling the assignment, and I had rarely had to wrestle with my conscience. But now I began to think of the human lives that had been lost, and I was sorry.

The nurses were talking in soft voices, and I strained to hear what they were saying. Luckily they spoke in English, and for the most part I could understand them. They were saying that I would live. They also mentioned that Kim Seung Il was dead.

I was devastated and felt a mixture of emotions. I was sorry that he was dead, for we'd been friends. I envied him being dead, because he would not have to face my inquisitors. And I was angry that he was dead, because I was now on my own and felt abandoned. Despite his ill health, Seung Il had always been a comforting presence because of his vast experience. I had relied on him during the many moments of uncertainty that we'd faced on our mission.

And then I did something for the first time in my life, something very strange: I prayed.

I was remembering a time, shortly before Bum Soo's death, when I had visited my home and found my mother placing bowls of water before a makeshift altar she'd constructed in her bedroom. This was an act of extraordinary courage, because in North Korea religion is strictly prohibited. My mother, in her desperate attempt to save her child, was driven to risk everything to ask for God's mercy.

And so I myself prayed. *Please, God, wherever you are, help me to die, right now. PLEASE.*

Even that act was rather painful. I was praying to a Being whom I didn't know.

What frightened me most was that if I remained alive, I was secretly doubtful that I could keep my identity and my mission a secret. And the moment I revealed these was the moment when I would forever become a traitor in the eyes of my leaders and my country. The fact that I had been captured did not in itself mean that the mission had failed. Kim Seung Il was dead, and he took his secrets with him to the grave. If I myself could remain silent, I could yet become the savior of North Korea.

But it was not North Korea that came to my mind. It was my

family. And I noticed that when I prayed to God for mercy, I had not, as had been my habit, prayed to the Great Leader, Kim Il Sung, who was the closest thing to a deity that I had ever known.

The hours passed. A Filipino nurse came to relieve the two on duty, and a female police officer had been stationed nearby. They were doubtless under orders to watch my every move and to keep me alive at all costs. They would not even let me fall asleep; I think they were afraid that I might relapse into a coma if I did so. If I so much as closed my eyes, the nurse would rush over and slap my face, whispering, "Mayumi! Mayumi!"

They seemed to like me, but I couldn't help thinking that they were only carrying out the orders of their superiors so that a confession could be extracted from me. My first reaction was to swear at them and tell them to leave me alone, but then I realized that the nurse and the policewoman were acting out of a simple desire to save a human life.

I regret now that I never expressed my gratitude for their kindness. I, a mass murderer, did not deserve to be kept alive. But they would not let me die, and I am sorry that I have only this book with which to convey my thanks to them.

As my senses returned to normal, I began to feel pain all over my body. My right knee in particular seemed to be badly injured, and I could not move it without excruciating pain. My mouth was full of blisters from the poison, and my tongue was so swollen that I could not swallow.

I began to have nightmares. I dreamed that my family was aboard Flight 858. I had placed the bomb in the overhead compartment and was shouting at them to get off the plane. Kim Seung Il, his skin blue and peeling away from his skull, gripped me with a skeletal hand and dragged me off the plane. I tried to break free, but his grip was too strong. I screamed hysterically to my family, who did not seem to understand what I was saying. At the end of the dream Kim dragged me to the door of the plane and threw me outside. As I plunged toward the runway, I woke up screaming.

"Mayumi!" The nurses rushed over, trying to calm me, but I sobbed and sobbed for hours.

In another dream I found myself on a snow-covered moun-

tainside. My family was coming up toward me, but they ignored me as if I were a stranger and merely passed me with
hostile or indifferent glances. Bum Soo, however, remained
behind, and he took my hand and suddenly we were jumping
into the sky, flying over the mountains like eagles. We began to
circle the crater of a volcano. Bum Soo, grinning at me, released
my hand, and as I plunged into the void, I again woke up
screaming.

I could not keep track of the time; I felt like I was in purga-
tory. Every now and then I would wake up, and there would be
a different nurse or policewoman sitting beside me. One nurse,
a black woman with beautiful brown eyes, washed my face and
combed my hair with such concern that I found my suspicion
and anger gradually melt away. She held my hand, saying,
"We are friends, Mayumi. I want you to believe that."

She left the room then, and two well-dressed men walked in.
I pretended to be asleep.

"Open your eyes. We know you are awake."

The language was Korean. I was so startled that I nearly
opened my eyes by reflex, but I managed to keep them shut.
My mind racing, I decided then and there that I could not
afford to admit my nationality. They repeated their command,
but I did not respond.

In actual fact I was glad to hear my native language, especially in that foreign country. This made silence all the harder.

Then a voice spoke in Japanese. I opened my eyes. One of
the two men was the Japanese who had detained us in the
airport; the other was a South Korean who had interrogated
Seung Il in our hotel room.

From that point on I responded only to questions in Japanese. The South Korean became impatient when I ignored his
requests and paced the room muttering to himself.

"Look," said the Japanese. "We need to get some information from you. We're trying to help you, Mayumi-*san*, but we
can't help you if you remain silent. All we want is your quick
recovery."

I nodded, but I knew that he was suspicious of me. His
sympathy was obviously feigned, and now and then I'd catch
him glaring at me. It became evident that I wasn't going to
cooperate with them, and at length they left the room.

I sighed. I had passed the first test, but it was only the beginning.

It was time, I realized, to try to think of a way out of this. I would watch for any chance to commit suicide, but in the meantime I needed to determine what I should tell them. I was still shaken from my first interrogation. I used the mind-control techniques that I had been taught and slowly resumed, psychologically at least, the composure of a special agent.

The best thing would be to pretend that I was a mute. I thought back, however, and realized that I had spoken or at least groaned in the presence of the nurses.

Since it was essential that I not speak Korean, I was left with a simple choice: Should I pretend to be Japanese or Chinese? My captors already knew that my Japanese passport was false, and there was also the question of my relationship to Seung Il.

I expected to be extradited to Japan. I had heard, through North Korean propaganda, that Japanese policemen were ruthless inquisitors and often resort to physical violence to extract confessions from their prisoners. I had also heard that they treated Koreans worst of all and tortured them with relish.

But even that would be better than going to South Korea. South Korean police, it was rumored, would gouge eyeballs from their sockets, knock out teeth, pull off fingernails. Perhaps that was why every North Korean agent who returned safely from an assignment in Seoul was regarded as a hero.

In any event I could not be Korean or Japanese, which left the choice of being Chinese. If they believed me, and I was extradited to China, I would probably be returned to Pyongyang, since the two governments were close allies. There was no direct evidence that I had been involved in the bombing, nor—it seemed at the time—could there ever be. As long as I made no concessions to my captors, things did not seem entirely hopeless.

I tried to think of a suitable background for myself. When Sook Hee and I had been stationed in Macao, we had assumed the identities of existing Chinese women. It seemed possible that I could use the name of one of those women—say, Pai Chui Hui—and give the biographical information of the second, Wu Eng, as my background. It wasn't foolproof, I knew; but I could think of nothing better to say.

My condition improved by the day. I was dressed in blue hospital pajamas and put into a wheelchair, to which I was handcuffed. The nurses washed me and took me to the bathroom, which was of course embarrassing. At no time, however, was I left alone, and the armed guards were stationed at my door around the clock. I began to drink some milky substance. Soon, I realized, I would be healthy enough to be interrogated formally.

It was for that moment that I braced myself.

Several days later—I can't say exactly how long—I was put into the wheelchair and taken to a police van outside the hospital. It was a beautiful day, warm and clear, and the sun was so bright that I could not open my eyes. It was the first time since my capture that I'd seen the outside, and the sight was rather depressing. It only confirmed what I had been thinking about in my hospital bed—that while *my* world was coming to an end, the rest of the world was continuing about its business unaffected. My face was covered with a veil, according to Arab fashion, and for a moment I thought that I would be executed. But they only lifted me into the van, which started off through the city.

Bahrain was a tropical paradise. I wanted only to go to the white beach and wade in the surf and forget that I had ever become a special agent and destroyed an airplane. I wanted to remember the days in Cuba, where I had once played in the water with my family and hadn't had a care in the world. But I was no longer a child now, and my parents could not rescue me. I was to be held accountable for my actions like any adult— and I would stand and die alone. I looked enviously at the innocent people walking along the street, a few feet away in distance, yet light-years away in circumstance. I felt consumed with envy of them.

We drove out of Manama into the countryside until we were on a deserted road. We reached some sort of police compound, surrounded by fences, with armed guards at the gates.

When the van stopped, I was taken inside to a small, drab room with a steel-framed bed and desk. I took one look at the place and knew that the serious part was about to begin.

I was thrown onto the bed and handcuffed to the frame. A moment later a middle-aged Caucasian couple entered the room. Both had blond hair and blue eyes, and they looked at me curiously but without malice. After a moment the man spoke in slow, deliberate English.

"My name is Ian Henderson," he said, "and this is my wife, Maria. I'm chief of police on Bahrain."

He went on to ask me how I was feeling. Maria stared at me with her large blue eyes, and for some reason I broke down under that gaze. As I cried, she pulled out a handkerchief and wiped the tears from my face.

"It's going to be all right, dear," she said, kissing me on the cheek. "Don't worry about a thing." She motioned to a pair of nurses who were standing nearby, and they adroitly removed my patient's garb and dressed me in blue Chinese pajamas. "She's beautiful," I heard one of them say, and I felt that they were just trying to torment me with feigned sympathy. *Just another ploy to get me to confess,* I thought. *I mustn't let down my guard, not for a moment.*

Henderson, as if sensing my thoughts, spoke again. "I suggest that you cooperate with us," he said. "This government doesn't think very highly of you, because you've hardly said a word to anybody."

I thought I detected a threat in his words. "What is it you want me to say?" I asked defiantly.

His face clouded. He was disappointed in me. "We'll be back tomorrow," he said, standing. "Think about what I said."

I do not recall how many days I stayed at the police station. As in the hospital, a nurse accompanied me everywhere. Everyone took a great interest in me, either for the gravity of my crime or because I was a young woman. At night three officers and a nurse were assigned to watch me. And though my wrist became swollen from the handcuff, and though my knee continued to ache, I never acknowledged the pain to my guardians. I was determined to salvage some last shred of dignity.

I underwent physical therapy every day, walking for two hours up and down the hall under the supervision of a doctor. I leaned on my nurse for support, and dragged my left leg most of the way. My pulse and temperature were taken every hour, and I was forced to eat and take medication.

One day, when they wanted to take a blood sample from my arm, I nearly went into hysterics. I had been told in North Korea that if captured, I might be injected with a truth serum that would compel me to reveal everything to my captors. The nurse was puzzled by my reaction and tried to comfort me. In the end she simply pinned down my arm and drew the blood.

I decided then that I could no longer remain silent. I would have to tell them something or I might be kept in this room forever. I began to ask for water and mentioned that my wrist hurt. The nurse, as well as the police who were guarding me, were ecstatic, and within moments the whole building knew that Mayumi had started to talk.

Henderson and his wife—I don't know what her function was, except perhaps to open me up—continued to visit the station every afternoon. They brought me clothes and cookies and did their best to make me feel at ease. They would talk about trivial subjects and then abruptly start asking about the bombing. Often I would not reply, or say that I knew nothing.

Finally, in exasperation, they handed me some written questions in Chinese, which I answered.

Q: What is your name?
A: Pai Chui Hui.
Q: What is your nationality?
A: Chinese.
Q: Your birth date?
A: January 27, 1964.
Q: Place of birth?
A: Heilong Jiang Province, Wuchang City, China.
Q: Your most recent address?
A: 4-10-6 Shibaya, Tokyo, Japan.
Q: Are your parents living?
A: No.
Q: Names of your brothers and sisters?
A: None.

I told them that I had been an orphan and had had nothing to do with the Korean Air disaster. "I don't understand why I'm being questioned about the incident," I said, hoping to turn the tables. "Is it a crime that I was on the plane?"

The more I told them, the less they seemed to believe. They always treated me with courtesy, however, and voiced concern about my physical condition.

One morning I was taken to the bathroom, without being asked if I wanted to go, and told to wash my face. I performed the job one-handed, like a cat. The nurse then squeezed some toothpaste onto a toothbrush for me, and I was told to brush my teeth. I felt strangely refreshed, and when I returned to my room, I was asked if I'd like some tea or coffee. I chose tea, suddenly nervous, and wondered what they were playing at.

The Hendersons came in when I'd finished my tea, bidding me a cheerful good morning. I was about to reply when I noticed a group of people right behind them. I shut my eyes, feeling a knot of dread in my stomach. They were reporters.

They began flashing their cameras as soon as they entered. I was ordered to follow their directions, and I posed as they asked me to. *Now my face will be on the front of every newspaper in the world,* I thought. *Everyone will be talking about the evil murderer who claimed 115 innocent lives.* My family would have no way of knowing, of course, although I remembered that in my mother's last letter she'd mentioned that my father would be spending a month in Angola on business. I could picture him walking into his hotel lobby, buying the morning paper, and seeing his daughter's face on the cover above the caption MURDERER.

No sooner had the reporters left than a pair of South Korean agents came in and examined every inch of my body, as though I were some zoo animal on display. I began to cry and covered my face with my hands. When the Koreans had gone, Henderson walked over to the bed and sat down.

"Why were you afraid of the South Koreans, Mayumi?"

"I wasn't," I snapped. "I just resented the way they treated me, that's all."

"So you weren't surprised by their appearance?"

"Why should I be surprised? You accused me of destroying a South Korean plane, so it seems obvious that South Koreans would be interested in me."

The next day I was visited by Japanese officials, who also tried to get me to talk. I had the feeling that they weren't absolutely sure I *was* Korean, so when I spoke, I tried to use perfect Japanese. I must have partially succeeded, because when they left, they were obviously unsure about me.

I sighed, exhausted but relieved. This was not going to get any easier. But even then I had no idea how hard it really would become.

My captors, perhaps reaching the end of their patience, brought in an interpreter from Hong Kong. She was English and a friend of Maria's and spoke fluent Cantonese. She introduced herself as Camilla, said that she was thirty-four, and told me that she had come to Bahrain two years ago with her husband, who was Chinese, and they owned a Chinese restaurant together. She was an attractive woman, and I envied her her simple, married lifestyle. In fact she seemed like the happiest woman I had ever met.

I started to cry before the interrogation even began, so their first questions were trivial and sympathetic.

"Now, Mayumi, suppose we start from the beginning," said Camilla when I had calmed down. "Where were you born?"

"I was born in Wuchang City. My father was an executive in a construction firm. He was found to be a traitor during the Cultural Revolution. He was tortured but released, though he committed suicide soon after that. My mother abandoned me and fled to Beijing to marry another man. At that point I was on my own." I started to cry again, because it was horrible that I could speak—even fictitiously—of my parents like that. The two women thought that I was grieving because of my lonely childhood, and they waited patiently for me to recover.

"I had no place to go," I continued. "Eventually I was taken in by my grandmother, who sold newspapers on the streets of Guangzhou, and I was able to get a job as a waitress. Then I met Comrade Wu Eng, a girl about my age, and together we fled to Macao with some young men who had stolen a boat."

They seemed to be buying the story. Even I was starting to believe it.

"I found work at a casino in Macao. There I met an elderly Japanese man named Shinichi Hachiya, who was very kind to me. When I told him of my circumstances, he offered to adopt me as his daughter if I'd return to Japan with him and become

125

his housekeeper. My life at that point was very difficult, and it seemed like a blessing. I couldn't return to China anyway, so I accepted his offer.

"His house in Tokyo was in the Shinbuyachu Ebishu district. He gave me the name Mayumi. He cared for me like a daughter but would not let me leave the house. He warned me that I might be arrested for not having a residence permit, so I rarely set foot outside. He promised to take me to Europe two or three times a year and possibly even America. We traveled to Europe a few weeks ago. He took care of the passports and the tickets. Now I find myself in this predicament. The only one who can corroborate my story is dead, and it seems like I'll have to suffer for a crime I didn't commit. I'll be taken to South Korea and tortured, and then they'll kill me!" I burst out sobbing, and to my surprise the other women were crying as well. Camilla asked if there was anything she could do to help, as if she was concerned that I would indeed be wrongly executed.

"Chui Hui," she said, using my "real" name for the first time, "you must insist on not going to South Korea. They will get a confession out of you, whether you're guilty or not."

"I know," I sobbed, feeling guilty that I was deceiving her, "but you won't let me go!" And I realized that although I had resolved to tell them nothing, their simple human kindness was somehow getting the better of me.

The interrogation ended at that point, and I was left alone with the guards. I fell into an uneasy sleep. Because I was having so many nightmares, I was afraid that I might say something in Korean while I was asleep. That night I had a dream that I was back in the Keumsung Military Academy and I was training for the two-kilometer swim. I was swimming across the lake, and the trainer, Park Ji Won, was rowing just ahead of me. I was swimming with all my strength without gaining an inch, and I started to sink. I began to gulp water, flailing desperately, and shouted to Ji Won. He turned his head, and it was my father, not Ji Won. He looked at me dispassionately and kept rowing, leaving me there to drown. *"Father!"* I screamed, using the last of my strength. *"Father, I'm drowning!"*

I woke up in a cold sweat, sobbing. The nurse was startled and reached over to comfort me. I continued to cry. I would

126

never see my father again, never. I would never be his little princess again.

The woman guard, several times a day, would play a set of chimes and then spread a *Shiratarsahlza*, a Persian rug that served as her prayer mat, on the floor. She would then face southwest and prostrate herself toward Mecca. To me it was a strange practice, praying to a god that one couldn't even see. North Koreans are taught from birth that religion is abhorrent, unnatural, and above all counterrevolutionary. We were told that religious practitioners are hypocrites, and I would react in contempt whenever I heard someone use the word *faith*. I felt that it was far superior and more rational to look to the Great Leader as our hero and inspiration, who was visible to us all the time. But I noticed the serene expression on the guard's face, the look of total piety, and I wondered whether North Koreans felt as reverent in front of Kim Il Sung's or Kim Jung Il's portrait.

For children this comes naturally, because they are encouraged to worship the Kims before they can even talk. But for adults it was not so easy. They worshiped the Kims for the sake of appearances. Their enthusiasm was largely feigned. They did not want to risk being deported, or worse, getting the club. For it is North Korean law that anyone who insults the Kim family is punished by being bludgeoned to death with an iron bar.

The guard finished her ceremony and rolled up her rug. She then walked over to me and held her arm against mine. "You must be Japanese, Mayumi, because your skin is so light. Look how dark mine is next to yours!"

I smiled, but was wary for any hidden intent on her part. She was only being friendly, but I knew that she thought I was a terrorist.

It became clear from Henderson's point of view that the interrogation was not proceeding as well as he'd hoped it would. His next tactic was to use a Japanese interrogator, and I recognized her from the hotel where Seung Il and I had stayed in Manama. I recalled that I had sometimes caught her looking at us in the lobby or following us on the street. I kicked myself for not realizing at the time that she was a spy.

The woman, whose name was Okubo, began questioning me about "Shinichi" and my stay in Japan, and I gave her the same answers I had Camilla. She interpreted my responses to Henderson, and his questions in turn to me.

Some contradictions began to appear in my story, because I could not keep track of what I had fabricated. I was asked to describe Shinichi's house and improvised an answer. They asked me about my schooling, my diet, my leisure activities. I suppose I should have shut up then, but I fumbled my way through the responses.

At one point Henderson motioned to Okubo to stop and looked at me thoughtfully.

"Chui Hui," said Henderson, speaking slowly, "you should know that there are presently a number of South Korean agents in Bahrain demanding that we release you into their custody. We're doing everything we can to help you. If you cooperate with us, we'll let you go back to China. But if you continue to lie to us, we'll have no alternative but to send you to Seoul. Think about it." He paused, making sure I understood, and then motioned Okuba to continue.

When the questioning turned to my trip to Europe, I was on easier ground. Henderson and I had become locked in a mental duel, one that I was gradually losing. When he asked about the boarding of Flight 858, I replied that the security had been airtight and that my body, as well as my luggage, had been searched.

Henderson above all did not believe that I was an orphan, because whenever the word *family* was mentioned, I usually began to cry. But I think the worst part came when they asked why I took the poison. Like a stupid, naive schoolgirl I answered, "Because Shinichi told me to."

Okubo then questioned me about how I felt toward Shinichi. I knew that this would eventually come up. I've already mentioned how Kim Seung Il was the perfect gentleman, but I was after all a mature young woman and I could see how other cultures might naturally suspect some romantic involvement between us. It was something that I in fact brought up to the section chief back in Pyongyang, before my first trip to Europe.

I was nervous about the trip in general and was far too modest a person to overlook such a detail. But when I brought it up to the section chief, he yelled at me: "Where are we going to get the money to afford *two* rooms?" He looked at me as though I had violated some ideological purity. I was a special agent; it was up to me to control my insecurities.

"You stayed in the same room while traveling. I suppose nothing happened between you?" Okuba asked.

"Of course not," I snapped. "He was like a father to me."

"Did you stay in rooms with a double bed or twin beds?"

"Twin."

"Where did you change your clothes?"

"In the bathroom."

"When you took a bath, did you lock the door?"

"Yes, dammit!"

"Have you seen Shinichi naked?"

My jaw dropped. *"What?"*

"For example," Okubo continued, without batting an eyelash, "did you ever notice the surgical scar on Shinichi's abdomen?"

"No, but I knew that he had had a stomach operation."

"Tell me," said Okubo, her eyes boring into me as Henderson watched, "have you had sex with other men besides Shinichi?"

I was so flabbergasted that I couldn't say anything. She took this as an admission of guilt and proceeded. "How many men have you had sex with?"

No response.

"Did you ever have an orgasm?"

No response.

"Did you ever seduce men as part of your job as a spy?"

No response.

"Was Shinichi the best lay you ever had?"

"Fuck you!" I shouted at her, in English, determined to beat her at her own game. "He was an old man, for God's sake!"

"Ah!" Henderson piped in. "So you're saying that he tried but was unable to?"

I stared at him, my blood boiling. I groped for a response, but I was so enraged that I could only, between deep breaths, sputter something incoherent.

"Too bad," said Okubo. "I understand from the autopsy that he was rather well endowed."

That did it. I jumped across the table before anyone could react and dealt her a classic martial arts blow—a palm-heel strike to the nose. I heard the cartilage crack, and blood spattered everywhere. Okubo screamed, falling back onto the floor. Henderson gave a shout and tried to subdue me, pinning my arms behind my back. I stamped on his toe with my heel, which loosened his grip, and delivered a hammer-fist punch to his groin followed by an elbow-strike to the side of his head. He was momentarily staggered. At once I frisked him, determined to shoot myself then and there. But the guards were already rushing at me from the doorway. I had just closed my hand around Henderson's pistol when I was pulled away from Henderson and seized in a headlock.

"Don't shoot her!" Henderson gasped. I saw him out of the corner of my eye, sagging against the wall, bent double. "That's what she wants! We need her alive!"

I knew my way out of a headlock. I chopped at my captor's groin, and simultaneously, as he released me, I used my other hand to reach up and grip his hair, pulling his head back viciously for a lethal blow to the neck. I drew my hand back for a knife-hand chop and at that moment was jolted as if by a stroke of lightning. I crumpled to the floor immediately, my whole body numb. I landed on my side, and looked up to see a second guard looming over me holding an electric stun gun. Before I could move, the third guard had cuffed my hands behind my back. I was helpless.

Henderson pushed himself to his feet. His face was flushed, his breathing heavy. He stared down at me with an expression of dazed loathing. "That's it, Mayumi," he rasped. "You've had your chance." He turned away, speaking to someone whom I couldn't see. "Get her out of here. She belongs to the South Koreans now."

CHAPTER TWELVE

THE PRISON TRANSPORT van sped to the airport through the twilit streets of Manama. A television had been set up in the van, tuned to the evening news. Although the broadcast was in Arabic, I could tell that the lead story was about South Korea.

Students, their faces covered with handkerchiefs, were throwing Molotov cocktails at lines of riot police. It seemed as though nothing less than a pitched battle was being waged in the streets of Seoul. Seeing this confirmed my belief that South Korean society was hopelessly fascist and far inferior to the socialist North.

It's the beginning of the end, I thought. Within hours I, too, would be in Seoul, and nothing would save me from the barbarities of the South Korean authorities.

Henderson sat next to me in the van, not saying a word. I knew that the news broadcast was a last-ditch ploy to get me to confess before I was sent away. Thinking back, I realized that everything that had happened in the jail had been toward the same intention. When Camilla had urged me to resist being transported to Seoul, she was merely playing on my fears. Since I believed that I would be mercilessly tortured in Seoul,

Henderson had seized the opportunity to use that against me. I recalled the gifts Maria had brought me—cookies, clothes, jewelry. I had been overwhelmed by her kindness, but then again I was intended to be. One of the things Maria had brought me was an athletic suit—matching sweatpants, sweatshirt, and nylon jacket. Everyone in North Korea wanted one of these. They were almost impossible to find in stores and were usually sold only on the black market. The nylon ones were especially coveted. It must seem alien to Westerners that such an item would be a major status symbol in North Korea. In 1987, as a gift to his nation, Kim Il Sung made them available for every child who attended middle school or high school. My mother rushed to buy one for Bum Soo, who died shortly thereafter. She knew he didn't have much time and wanted to make him happy. He was enthralled by the gift and would keep it next to his head so that he could touch it personally. He would smile thankfully at my mother as he drifted in and out of consciousness. He died holding the suit in his hand. He never even had a chance to wear it.

So when Maria brought me such a suit, I could not help but feel grateful. At the same time I expected that I would soon be executed and that the suit was some last act of generosity before I was taken to the firing squad. In my position I always had to question the motives of my captors, and often any attempt of mine at cool, detached reasoning was compromised by simple emotional turmoil.

This was the suit I was wearing in the van, the suit I would wear when I disembarked in Seoul. It seemed like a strange piece of symbolism at the time.

Maria also rode in the van, along with four guards. She often looked at me in pity, but said nothing. There was nothing left to say between us, although I did want to thank her for her kindness. When the nurses had dressed me for the journey—I could tell they were fighting back tears—Maria had stood nearby, her face unreadable. She must have been greatly disappointed in me, but I suspect she felt empathy as well.

After the incident in the jail the guards were no longer kind to me. When the van was ready, they marched me outside, their arms interlocked with mine, and roughly they threw me inside. I noticed that there would be two police cars accompanying us. I would have my own convoy of sorts to see me off from Bahrain.

It was dark by the time we reached the airport. We drove directly toward the docking bays, past aircraft-maintenance vehicles and a series of guidance lights. At the sound of the plane engines my heart began to pound, and my face broke out in a cold sweat. This was it.

The van stopped. I was lifted outside and found a Korean Air jet towering over me like an enormous metallic monster. I was now overcome by sheer terror, a fear far greater than anything I'd experienced until now. I let out a scream and began struggling with the guards, but they were far too strong. My hands were bound, and I was too off-balance to use my feet. They pulled me toward the stairs that led up to the plane's entrance. At the bottom of the stairs stood two South Korean agents, their faces blank. They deftly took me from the Bahraini guards and shoved something in my mouth, then sealing it with adhesive tape. It was some plastic device that prevented me from biting my tongue.

The Koreans lifted me into the airplane like a piece of luggage. I was marched into the middle of the cabin and shoved into a seat. A male and female agent sat on either side of me, their arms still interlocked with mine. I was sobbing by this time, and a third agent cleaned off my face. He muttered something in an attempt to comfort me when the agent seated to my left—the woman—intervened.

"Just leave her alone and let her calm down herself."

I might as well be dead, I thought, not knowing that there was a lot worse to come.

Within moments of my new captivity I made my first and most decisive mistake. Another agent had walked up to me and was examining my hands. "These are the hands of a trained spy," he said to the agents seated next to me. "See how she keeps them open like this?"

I immediately squeezed my hands shut. I had just, without even realizing it, confirmed that I understood Korean.

The plane took off without any formal announcement. There were no flight attendants; this trip had been arranged just for me. There was a certain irony to this, that one North Korean should have an entire flight to herself. The vast majority of North Koreans never traveled abroad at all. To do so, one needed a "hook"—a popular slang term, like "pulling strings," that referred to having special connections with Kim Il Sung's family.

Outside there was pure darkness, but the cabin lights were left on. No one would be sleeping on this flight, least of all me.

I tried to ascertain what they already knew: that I was carrying a false Japanese passport, that I had tried to commit suicide, and that I was a trained martial artist. None of these linked me directly to the bombing, but I would have been a fool not to see a certain pattern emerging that clearly pointed to my guilt.

"Are you uncomfortable?" asked the woman next to me in Japanese.

"Speak to her in Korean," said the other agent, the man sitting to my right.

But whenever they spoke in Korean, I pretended not to understand, and the woman would occasionally whisper things in Japanese.

The flight seemed to last forever. I could think only of the various ways in which I'd be tortured when we arrived in Seoul. Water torture, scorpions, white hot pokers—these were only a few of the methods that the South Koreans were rumored to employ. I spent the entire flight shaking, and even when they threw a blanket around my shoulders I shivered uncontrollably. At one point I heard an agent say, "For someone who committed such an atrocity, doesn't she look like a princess sleeping in a forest?" I thought it was nonsense, but later I learned that he had been alluding to "Snow White." This meant nothing to me at the time, since all Western literature was banned in North Korea and the only children's books were devoted solely to the glory of Kim Il Sung. Once, in training camp, a field agent had smuggled a copy of *Tales from a Thousand and One Nights*, which the rest of us read in fascination and awe.

To pass the time and maintain my resolve, I kept repeating a song in my head called "March of the Commandos."

Comrades, prepare the arms held in your hands
Destroy the imperialist invaders
Forward and forward we bravely march
Destroy the enemies if it takes a thousand deaths.

Let us march to the showdown
Let us march to the battlefield
As we hold our arms firmly in our hands
Forward and forward we bravely march
Destroy the enemies even if it takes a thousand deaths.

I also thought of my family. I recalled the time my maternal grandmother had come to see me several months earlier during my last trip home. I had not seen her in fifteen years, and she wept with joy when she saw me.

"Oh, Hyun Hee," she said, embracing me tightly, "my life has been worth living just to see you again. All through the years I kept seeing your face."

That night we had a Korean delicacy, Shinshullo, and the mood was festive as we spoke of the "good old days." Hyun Ok, recently married, had stopped by to visit.

Later that evening there was a frantic knock on the door. My mother answered. A young man, dripping with sweat, stood outside looking distraught. He proceeded to tell us, in an unsteady voice, that Hyun Ok's husband had died that day of a heart attack while swimming in Changgwangwon. As part of his work for the tourist agency he used to take visitors swimming in Pyongyang's largest swimming facility. Although young, he had been complaining of fatigue for some days, and Hyun Ok had been urging him to take it easy.

Now he was dead. And Hyun Ok, barely twenty years old, was a widow. Our living room, which had been full of laughter, became a funeral home.

With a start I came to my senses. Daylight streamed through the windows, and I could tell that the plane was descending rapidly. My heart began to pound all over again as I heard a voice say, "We're coming up on Seoul."

CHAPTER THIRTEEN

THE PLANE HIT the runway with a jolt. When we had slowed down, an agent strode over to me with a fur coat.

"It's cold outside," he said. "Put this on."

I was allowed to stand, and the handcuffs were unlocked. I slipped into the fur coat, and then my hands were cuffed again.

The plane stopped. One of the doors was pulled open, and a blast of cold air hit me. It was quite a contrast from tropical Bahrain. There was something about the scent of the air that put me in mind of Pyongyang, and for a moment I thought we'd actually landed at Soonan Airport. But then I reached the door and looked outside. This was not Soonan.

The size of the airfield was staggering. There were dozens of planes in sight, taking off every minute. The airport was as large as any I'd seen in Europe.

I could see that a throng of reporters had gathered on the ground below, cameras ready. A mobile staircase was being wheeled to the door of the plane. I shut my eyes, as if doing so would allow me to vanish from this dreadful place.

I was led down the stairs. I could hear the camera clicking, and there was a babble of excitement among the reporters.

136

"She's beautiful!" I heard one man exclaim. "How could anyone so beautiful be a terrorist?"

The agents who were leading me stopped for a moment to let the photographers have their chance. Everyone was calling for me to look in their direction, and I became so flustered that I burst into tears. Not for the first time I felt like a piece of merchandise on display.

"Hey, baby, calm down!" I heard someone yell. "You're in Seoul!"

At length I was pushed into a waiting limousine, which sped away. I was dazed and sat with my head bowed and my eyes shut. I could not stop crying.

"Why don't you look outside?" one of the agents asked. "Aren't you curious about Seoul?"

In truth I was. Despite its alleged poverty, violence, and corruption, Seoul was held in awe by North Koreans. In the event of reunification, Seoul would be the jewel in the crown. But I was so overwhelmed with exhaustion and fear at that point that I couldn't bear to look.

"Is anyone still following us?" one of the agents asked the driver.

"No, we've lost them all."

"Excellent. Proceed to Namsan."

We would move at high speed for a time and then stop altogether. All the while I could hear the sounds of many other cars on the road around us. Had I looked, I would have seen—and been astonished—that the drivers were Koreans. But at the time, with my head bent down and my eyes closed, I assumed that with so many cars on the streets, Seoul had been taken over by foreigners.

I felt like a cow being led to the slaughterhouse, and I was anxious to reach our destination. By that time I was so tired of living that the thought of death was more welcome than ever. And then I realized something. The agent had said "Namsan"; he must have meant the infamous Namsan interrogation complex, which had become legendary among North Korean spies. Rumor had it that there was a chamber in the basement where the most unspeakable acts of torture were committed. No North Korean had ever returned from Namsan.

I began to feel faint, and I think I might have passed out. I remember that when I came to my senses, the car had stopped, and the doors were being opened.

Oh no, I am here. What will it be for me? The water torture, where they pour water into your stomach until it bursts? The sex torture, where they take a wooden spike and . . .

"We're here," said the female agent next to me. "You can rest now."

I was led into a small room and made to lie down. A doctor examined me, and I heard him say, "Everything appears to be normal, but she's overly exhausted. She should sleep for a while."

"Agreed. But give her a glucose injection first. Her blood sugar is probably low."

I shut my eyes as the needle was inserted, thinking that it must be a truth serum. I felt momentarily jumpy, but soon settled into an uneasy sleep.

When I woke, I could hear voices arguing next door. Although my door was shut, I could hear them through the walls quite clearly.

"We're wasting time, that's why!" a man shouted. "We should remove the mouthpiece immediately and start the interrogation!"

"It's far too dangerous!" yelled a woman in reply. "The Director hasn't given us permission yet!"

"Look, I'll take responsibility," the man snapped. "We've got to do it at some point."

The voices subsided, and a few minutes later a male investigator came in to remove the plastic gag. My mouth was dry and my throat hurt, but the worst pain was from the adhesive tape. The investigator ripped it off, taking some skin in the process, but I did not cry out. I had been a wreck since leaving Bahrain, and I thought that it was time I showed some courage.

I opened my eyes for the first time since the airport. The room was painted all in white and had no windows. Besides the bed, there were two desks, a sofa, and some chairs. I felt the gooseflesh on my skin as I looked around, wondering how many of my country's patriots and revolutionaries had been killed in this room before me.

Three more people came into the room. There were now two male and two female agents. I tried to summon my psychological defenses to prepare for the mental combat that I knew would soon take place. The agents spoke politely, but their eyes missed nothing. They were trained professionals, the South Korean equivalent of the KGB or CIA.

I was forced to drink some milky substance and soon after fell into a deep sleep. When I woke, they were still there, and indeed seemed not to have moved at all. A man and a woman sat at each desk, studying me and making notes. The other woman stood at the foot of the bed, while the fourth agent leaned against the wall by the door. There were sounds of activity from outside, and I wondered whether it was morning. After a while the woman at the foot of the bed told me to get up. I tried to comply, but I was too weak and had to be supported. She led me out of the room and down the hall to a bathroom, where I was stripped naked and washed thoroughly. I was embarrassed at being so exposed, but the hot water soothed me. My captors were being very gentle, and I of course began to suspect that this was all a ploy to win my confidence. I noted smugly that the shampoo and soap were foreign-made. In the North we produced such goods for ourselves, though the quality was not first-rate.

I was then permitted to brush my teeth, which I had not done since Bahrain. When I was finished, I was given a new set of clothes. All carried South Korean labels, and the underwear and training suit that were provided were of far superior quality to anything I had ever worn before. Why, I asked myself, should they waste such expensive clothing on a criminal, if not to trick me into confessing?

When I returned to the room, I was given a cup of coffee. I had been craving one for days. It was scalding hot, and I was forced to blow the steaming vapor from the surface. One of the agents remarked to another, "I am sure that she is Korean. Only Koreans blow off the steam like that." Before I could stop myself, I had set down the cup.

Bastards!

I stood and took the cup into the adjoining bathroom and threw out the coffee. As I was washing out the cup, a female agent wandered in and told me to throw it away. I was puzzled. I was holding a perfectly good paper cup that could be used again. It seemed a terrible waste and confirmed to me that South Korea was a poor, debt-ridden nation.

I was then given a huge breakfast of eggs, rice, and kimchi, the spiced cabbage that is a national addiction. I tried not to eat, but soon the delicious aromas got the better of me and I gobbled everything down. As I did so, I asked, in Japanese, what the date was. I was told that it was December 17, seventeen days since the incident in Bahrain. That seemed about right, and I wondered how long I could hold out.

I made another decisive mistake when I overheard two female agents wondering about my menstrual period. Since it would have to be taken care of, I wrote "24" on a piece of paper—meaning that I expected it December 24. They didn't seem to pay much attention to it at the time, and then their conversation turned to the election.

"Who did you vote for?"

"Well, our household was divided along gender lines. The men want X, the women want Y. So I'm voting for Y."

I didn't understand any of this. I came from a country where we considered ourselves lucky to have one strong candidate—Kim Il Sung—who was invariably "elected" to the presidency. The whole notion of "freedom of choice" seemed unnecessarily chaotic, and I wondered how South Koreans ever agreed on anything.

Elections are held in North Korea every four years. For each regional position there is only one candidate, who is selected by the Labor Party, and the people vote either yes or no. For weeks before the election, rallies are held, parades organized, and seminars held to encourage one-hundred-percent voter participation. Of course everyone over seventeen is required by law to vote anyway, so all the encouraging slogans and festivities are a sham.

When Election Day arrives, people queue up at the polls at seven A.M. to vote. There is usually a band playing nearby to enliven the spirit of the occasion. A voter, after being registered, is given a piece of paper on which an "affirmative" vote is stamped. The voter then proceeds into a hallway where three election officials are seated and approaches the portraits of the Kim family and bows. He or she then places the "affirmative" vote in the box beneath the portraits. To vote no, an individual would have to refrain from placing the paper in the box. Needless to say, with the election officials looking right at you it is unthinkable to dissent.

I was given lunch, which consisted of rice porridge and dried seaweed. This is a Korean delicacy, but I was supposed to be Chinese; so I asked my captors if the seaweed was burnt paper. They smiled but said nothing and instead began telling jokes among themselves.

"What person keeps talking whether or not anyone listens?"

"A politician?"

"Close. A schoolteacher."

Or:

"A certain judge asked a burglar why he kept stealing. The burglar replied that he was hungry. When the judge pointed out that he had just stolen a pair of shoes, the burglar said, 'Well, I can't steal in bare feet!' "

Or:

"A Russian is deported to Siberia for unpatriotic conduct. He says to the judge, 'Hey, if America is as bad as you say, why not send me there instead?' "

I had to race to the bathroom to suppress my laughter. To a Korean that sort of joke was hilarious, and even in my circumstances I was somehow not immune. I turned on the water to cover up my giggles. It was the first time I had laughed in weeks.

The South Korean agents were true professionals. They treated me with the utmost respect. They knew that doing so would bring quicker results than any physical violence or direct questions. By simply being forced to live among them, I, a fellow Korean, was slowly but inevitably breaking down.

One day the female agents suggested that we all sing songs instead of sitting around and doing nothing. A woman named Park Lin started with a song that I recognized: "Mountain Bunny." It was the sort of plainsong that had been banned by Kim Jung Il and replaced with nationalist propaganda. As I listened, fascinated, I felt images of my childhood rushing into my head:

The Village where I lived was in a flowering valley in the
　　hills.
Peaches, apricots, and baby azaleas were in full bloom,
Adorning my village in bright colors like a palace.
I long for the days when I played in the palace in full bloom.

I sang privately with her. I recalled my grandmother's house in Gaesung, a traditional shingle-roofed house set in beautiful hills with a brook running past the front door. In the spring the azaleas would be in full bloom, carpeting the valley in a brilliant red, just like in the song.

Next it was my turn to sing. I sang a popular Chinese song called "Plum Blossom":

Plum blossom, plum blossom everywhere,
The colder it gets, the brighter they bloom.
Plum blossom resisting the winter
Symbolizes our spirit.
Plum blossom, plum blossom, great flower of China.

When I finished, a male agent spoke in Japanese. "Why don't you sing a Korean song instead, since you're in Korea now? It's only polite, you know."

The rest of the agents clapped their hands and encouraged me. I protested that I didn't know any Korean songs, but they continued to press me. At last I gave in and hummed a few bars of a song I'd seen on television, which delighted them. It seemed better than refusing to participate altogether.

Next a woman sang a hauntingly beautiful song in Korean:

Bells are ringing, flowers are blooming.
The birds are singing, faces are smiling.
I yearn for my love in beautiful Seoul,
In beautiful Seoul I shall live.

The song broke something within me. I found myself wondering if Seoul was indeed beautiful, and from the expressions of the agents it seemed possible that it was. But then I admonished myself. Where was the revolutionary spirit that I had developed for the past eight years? Where was the single-minded devotion to my country? I was allowing myself to be seduced by these people, and I felt powerless to resist.

The investigators eventually started asking casual questions about my background, although there was no formal interrogation. They did so in a conversational way, as if I was among friends, and I gave them the same story that I had told Henderson in Bahrain. They seemed to believe me and said nothing aggressive or challenging, and occasionally made some notes. To some of their questions I had to grope for answers.

"Can you think of any movie stars from the films you saw in Macao?"

"Bruce Lee."

"Did you bite the poisoned ampule because Shinichi told you to?"

"Um . . ."

"If you are Chinese, you must have met a lot of Koreans. Are you saying that you don't know a single word of Korean?"

"Er . . . *Gan Na* [bitch]."

One of the agents held a photograph of Kim Il Sung in front of me. "Have you ever seen this person?"

I gazed at it thoughtfully. "I think so, on TV."

"What's his name?"

"Jin Reu Chung," I replied, using Chinese pronunciation.

Later that night, as I was trying to fall asleep, I heard them talking in low voices.

"It's unforgivable to use a girl like that as a political tool."

"I know. A crime is a crime, but I really feel sorry for her."

"It's that bastard Kim Il Sung who deserves to be punished."

At that moment I wanted to leap out of bed and shout, "You sons of bitches! How dare you call the Great Leader a bastard?" In my country there was no greater heresy. To North Koreans Kim Il Sung was like the sun to the earth. But of course I could do nothing.

The next day—December 18—they began to interrogate me in earnest. They were polite but thorough, and they asked for details that, try as I might, I couldn't hope to supply. They wanted to know street names where I had supposedly grown up. They wanted to know the names of movie theaters that I had attended. They asked me to draw Shinichi's house and asked endless questions about my stay in Japan. As I had never been to Japan, there was no way I could fabricate answers that were remotely plausible. All the while they would converse in Korean among themselves, making observations about me. "This girl is too stupid to be a spy," one of the men would remark, watching to see how I would react.

The next day was a nightmare. A new investigator was brought in, a handsome man in his fifties who wore a stylish black suit and chain-smoked American cigarettes. He asked me, in Chinese, to draw a flowchart of my entire life history, with names, dates, and significant events. "We know you're Korean," he remarked as I worked. "It would be easier to admit it now."

I ignored him and finished the diagram, which I pushed across the desk. He looked at it and smirked before crumpling it up and tossing it into a wastebasket. "This girl is obviously lying," he said in Korean to the other agents.

And I, at that point, demanded in Chinese, "What I am lying about?"

He looked at me, eyebrows raised mockingly, as if to say, "Need I say more?" He lit a fresh cigarette and studied me.

"Tell me," he said, expelling smoke through his nostrils, "what sort of TV did you watch in Japan? I mean, what was the brand?"

"Azalea."

He smirked, and the other agents broke into laughter. Azalea was a North Korean brand, but by this point I was confused and angry that I couldn't think straight anymore.

"What station did you usually watch?" he asked.

"Look," I snapped, standing up, "I'm tired of answering all these questions. Why do you keep asking me the same questions over and over? If you think I'm guilty, then *why don't you fucking shoot me??!*"

I threw myself on my bed and cried. I was not worthy to be called a special agent. I had none of the mental resolve and analytic dexterity that the profession so obviously required. I just wanted to go home, and be with my family, and forget that

I had ever been selected by the Party. I wanted Bum Soo to be alive again. And I wanted to die.

Their questions day by day became even tougher. They asked how much Shinichi used to pay me, how much of it I saved, and the name of the bank where I held an account. They asked if I had ever taken a Japanese taxi, and when I replied yes, they asked me to draw the seating arrangement. Did I know the color of the airport terminal in Narita? Did I know how many stories it was? Had I ever been to a place in Guangzhou called Shawmen?

They asked me to write my name. I wrote Pai Chui Hui in Chinese characters. They took the paper and left the room, and a few moments later came back with my name printed in many different sizes. It was my handwriting; and yet how had they made my name appear as small as a sesame seed and as large as a street sign? I gaped at the paper, utterly at a loss. They were amused by my reaction but said nothing more about it and instead asked me a question that sent chills up my spine.

"Whom did you meet in the Baghdad airport? There was more than one person, wasn't there? Does the name Choi mean anything to you?"

The question was asked in Korean. But it surprised me so much that I could not mask my reaction. My eyes widened, and I think my face went white.

"This is getting tedious, isn't it?" the investigator asked in Chinese. "This is getting tedious, isn't it?" he repeated in Japanese. "THIS IS GETTING TEDIOUS, ISN'T IT?" he practically shouted in Korean, and I broke down in tears.

He thrust my passport in my face. "Who is this person?" he demanded.

I stood and knocked the passport from his hand. "How the fuck should I know?" I screamed at him, my hands balling into fists.

He closed in on me, and I was backed against the wall. His face was hard as stone. When he spoke in Korean, his voice was a quiet hiss. "There were one hundred and fifteen people aboard that plane. Most were innocent workers, with no political connections whatsoever. They worked their asses off in that boiling-hot desert to feed and clothe their families and to give an education to their children. They had been away from home for months and were returning with the money they had knocked themselves out to earn. We don't know why you did it, but you deserve to be struck by *lightning* for what you have done." He paused, taking a puff of his cigarette, and blew a stream of smoke in my face. "I know you didn't act alone and that you were probably put up to it against the price of your life, at least subtly. But damn it, you *owe it* to the families of those victims to confess so that we can act against those who were truly responsible for this crime. If we lose the essence of our humanity, what more are we than mere animals in the wild; mad, uncivilized beasts?"

By this point I was sobbing uncontrollably, but he was not through yet.

"You've just about lost your humanity, young woman," he continued, jabbing a finger at me. "How can we be expected to treat you as a human being? Why should we? There is a season for everything, and the time for penitence is slipping away. If you let the chance go by, you may never be granted another."

His eyes bore into mine. His face, so close to mine, was not nearly as handsome now.

"Your government has little regard for human life, and I regret that you were one of their pawns. If you had done something noble, there might have been some honor due to you. But taking innocent lives is not honorable. It's evil and it's damned foolish. And you, not realizing just how foolish it was, are all the more foolish yourself. Do you understand? One who turns from justice to wrongdoing is called a traitor or a turncoat. But one who turns from evil to goodness is called righteous. To brainwash a young girl is a despicable thing. There is yet time for you, young woman, to ask for forgiveness and seek redemption for what you have done. But that time, I can tell you, is running out." He held my gaze for a moment and then turned away. But even now he wasn't finished. When he reached the door, he turned and delivered one more parting shot.

"You can think of it like this: You can confess and give absolution of a sort to the families who have lost their loved ones. Or you can die with the blood of one hundred and fifteen innocent lives on your hands, for a country that cares no more for your life than that of a fly. Not even God would want to save you then." He stepped into the hallway, but I heard his voice even as he walked away. "Think about it, Chui Hui. Or should I say Ok Hwa?"

CHAPTER FOURTEEN

I WAS DEFEATED.

For two weeks of relentless interrogation in Bahrain, and for eight days of even more intense questioning in Seoul, I had resisted them. With every bit of cleverness I could muster I had lied to be faithful to Our Great Leader. I had lied again to cover up those lies. And above all, I had lied to save my family from what I knew would be their certain doom.

But that was over now. My resistance had been exhausted. The South Koreans had beaten me. It had taken no violence on their part, as I had expected; only infinite, reasonable patience. I had told them that I was a Chinese orphan. I had told them that I had been informally adopted by the kindly Shinichi Hachiya and was traveling with him on vacation to Europe. But I could not deceive them. They knew perfectly well that I was a North Korean spy, even before I confessed to it. They also knew it was I who had caused the deaths of 115 innocent people, for which I could never be forgiven.

Yes, I was beaten. And in the end, of all things, it was the city of Seoul that pushed me beyond the last stand of resistance. I had been raised to believe that South Koreans were

148

poverty-stricken puppets of a ruthless capitalist regime. And when I first came to Seoul, I desperately wanted to believe what I had been taught.

But I had been reborn. The child who had grown up a disciple of Kim Il Sung had died in the Bahrain airport. Slowly, gradually, a different person was taking her place. And Seoul, more than anything, was the parent of this new child.

It was the day before I finally confessed. My guardians told me that we would take the day off from their interrogation and go sightseeing in the city.

I was given a two-piece black suit to wear. I felt like a little girl at her first day of school all dressed up like that, and I wondered why they were treating me so kindly.

When we drove outside the police compound, we proceeded up a hillside. The trees were familiar, the granite rocks and red soil were familiar . . . nothing seemed out of place. The sky above me—a deep blue sky, with a single white floating coat— this was the same sky I saw in Pyongyang. But then we reached the crest of the hill, and I saw downtown Seoul spread out before me like a marvel. My illusion of being in the Korea I knew was shattered.

There was a flood of automobiles. Not even in Western Europe had I seen so many cars, jostling in the broad streets. Shocked, I studied the drivers. They were Koreans, not foreigners.

For a moment I couldn't speak. The spectacle was so different from what I had expected that I didn't know what to say. "I don't believe it," I finally managed to whisper.

A special agent riding with us gestured at the traffic. "All these cars are made in Korea," he said to me. "Most families have their own car these days; they say even a beggar uses a car for his rounds. What this all means is traffic congestion and a shortage of parking space. These are serious social problems."

Our car lurched stop-and-go, stop-and-go with the others. I understood the import of his last sentence, but I was also mindful of his earlier words. In North Korea only high-ranking Party officials or government ministers drove cars, and we students used to bow as they passed. To become a driver was one of the most coveted professions among young people, at least among men. Women wouldn't dream of driving cars; they were sometimes allowed to operate trolley buses, but that was as far as they could go.

And yet here in Seoul I noticed that many of the drivers were women. I was so overwhelmed that I could only lean my forehead against the window and stare.

We drove through South Gate, the City Hall, the capitol, the Olympic Village, the Trade Center in Jamsil. I was impressed by everyone's uninhibited manners, their animated expressions, their colorful clothes. But what struck me most were the roadside peddlers, whom I spotted at every stoplight. In the North I had been told that roadside peddlers were the lowliest people in the South. But the merchandise they were selling was anything but lowly—expensive watches, high-quality tools, elegant clothes and shoes. Never could this have been possible in North Korea, where the price of a single watch could feed a family of five for seven months. The peddlers here looked as though they were earning a fortune from their sales. How could they be called poor?

At nightfall we drove up Namsan Mountain so that I could see the lights of the city spread out below me. The sight was so beautiful, and I knew that I had fallen in love.

Agreeing to drive out into Seoul had been my last mistake, and also my liberation. My captors must have anticipated the effect that it would have on me. I couldn't shake the feeling that the first twenty-six years of my life had been something of a sham.

I felt a surge of hatred for Kim Il Sung as I realized in one brief moment that all my work and plans and training, indeed my entire life, had been founded upon lies.

The next morning I was again sitting across the interrogation table from the special agent who had lectured me two nights before. He asked politely how I had enjoyed my outing the previous day and smiled when I could think of nothing adequate to say.

"I am going to point out your lies one by one. Listen hard, think carefully, and don't lie. There is only one truth, and we already know what it is. Do you understand?"

He paused, lit a cigarette, and continued.

"You are absolutely not a Chinese. Why? You said you lived in Wuchang City for fifteen years. But there is no Wuchang City as such, only a county called Wuchang-hsien. And if you indeed grew up in the north, as you say you did, you would know that the word *tungsu* [to become mature] is used only in southern China. You yourself used this word many times. You also referred to the corn porridge as *wuimei*, which is another southern term. The northerners use the term *paomei*, which you failed to mention even once.

"You also said that you grew up a wandering orphan and that your staple food was Hoppang bread. As it happens, that bread is consumed only by rich people. And when you stated that an aunt of yours in Wuchang peddles newspapers and dumplings on the street, you apparently did not realize that newspapers are not sold on the streets of Wuchang County."

He paused again, allowing me to digest this. "There are many more such contradictions," he continued. "All these point to one thing: You are not Chinese, and it's pointless to keep pretending you are."

He lit a fresh cigarette, never taking his eyes from me. As he exhaled the smoke, he went on. "You claimed that you lived in Japan for a year with Mr. Hachiya. Yet when you were served toasted seaweed, a Japanese delicacy, you asked sarcastically if it was burnt paper." He seemed amused by this, and the others in the room snickered. "Do you remember the sketch you drew of Shinichi's residence in Japan? That sketch in no way resembled a Japanese house, and the streets that you sketched had no similarities to Japanese streets either.

"You claimed to watch television often, and yet when asked the brand of Shinichi's set, you called it a Jindalrae, the Korean word for azalea. Jindalrae happens to be a North Korean brand, as I think you secretly know. Moreover, the Seoul Asian games were telecast in Japan every day during the period when you supposedly lived there, and yet you didn't know which country was the winner.

"You said that in a Japanese taxi, the driver's seat is on the left, when in fact it is on the right. And lastly, if you had left Japan on November fourteenth, as you claimed, you would have known that their prime minister had been replaced. But you said it was Nakasone instead of Takeshita—a decisive error.

"So," he concluded, stubbing out his cigarette, "after all those contradictory statements—and I assure you, there were a great deal more—how can you possibly claim to have lived in Japan?"

It was as though a noose was being tightened around my neck. I had no lies left to tell them and bowed my head. But the interrogator wasn't finished with me.

"We've been watching you closely since your arrival, literally every move you've made. And we noticed, for example, how expertly you handled your bedding, as though you'd had prolonged and systematic military training.

"You claim not to understand Korean. So when we noticed that you habitually tapped your fingers during these interviews, we said, in Korean, 'Finger tapping is a sign of nervousness.' You instantly stopped moving your fingers. When we talked among ourselves in Korean, and said, 'Oh, listen to her, she's lying,' you tried harder than ever to convince us you were telling the truth. And when we told jokes in Korean, you had to rush to the bathroom to stop yourself from laughing.

"And then there was the final test." His face hardened, and he leaned forward, eyes probing. "When I handed you a written statement in Korean that said, 'You are a North Korean spy,' I saw the instant look of embarrassment and fear in your face. Shall I continue?"

I felt as though I had been stripped, garment by garment. No, there was no need for him to go on; I couldn't stand to hear any more. I was ashamed, angry, humiliated, sorry . . . in short I was completely beaten, and knew I could resist no further. And silence could not save my life any longer.

But what would happen if I revealed my secret? Death, certainly, for I was a murderer. But what about my family? I recalled a high school friend of mine, Ku Jahyang, whose family had had a black-and-white television set and always seemed to have candy in the house. I used to spend many nights at her house, because we could watch the TV and eat caramels. Her younger brothers were excellent students and Youth Corps leaders in their schools.

One day, in 1974, Ku Jahyang did not show up for school. The gossip was that a younger brother had reported to the Social Security Department that his mother was a spy. An investigation was conducted, with the result that both her parents and an uncle were accused of being spies. Soon the whole family was expelled to a concentration camp in Yanggang-do, and their neighbors worried about being deported as well for being associated with them.

I had heard what those camps were like—day after day, year after year of back-breaking labor. I did not want my brother and sister and parents to go through that.

In North Korea the wives used to worry about their husbands drinking too much, and not because of their health, like everywhere else. Instead they were afraid that their husbands would say something foolish and be reported for it. One wrong word and the whole family could be ruined.

Such was life in North Korean society, and it was plain as day what would happen to my family once I confessed. I could see images of my father and mother, of Hyun Soo and Hyun Ok, being arrested by the Secret Police and taken away.

Doubts began nagging at my mind. Had my mission really been worthwhile? Did my terrible actions, and the deaths they caused, really contribute toward Korean reunification? Would the country continue to remain divided if Seoul did not host the Olympic Games? And would the destruction of a single airplane really have prevented them from being held in Seoul?

Slowly it dawned on me that unless one was an idiot, it was obvious whose stance was more reasonable.

And so at this point only one obstacle remained between myself and a full confession—my family. If I remained silent to the death, they would live out the rest of their lives in honor. And yet . . .

And yet would they? The South Koreans already knew much, and it was certainly possible that they could piece together the rest of my story on their own. There would be no bargaining with them—they would not accept taking my life quietly to spare my family's, and they could make the story public at any time they chose.

Something else occurred to me as well. Did I not owe it to the families of the victims to confess? Did I not have at least to admit, with total honesty and repentance, the atrocity of my actions, in order for me to be considered anything less than a monster? Yes, for these people deserved nothing less.

I looked up at the investigator. Slowly I made myself say the words. "Forgive me, I am sorry. I will tell you everything."

CHAPTER FIFTEEN

I FELT EMPTY.

In the aftermath of my confession I could only lie back on my bed in a daze. I was physically and emotionally numb. By confessing I had shrugged the world from my shoulders, but now I was floating in empty space, without anchor or direction. Half conscious, enervated and depressed, I expected that I would soon be executed, but the thought made little impression on me. I was beyond feeling anything at this point, and I didn't care what happened to me.

It had taken eight hours to reveal the whole story. They now knew almost as much about me as I did myself. I noticed from an investigator's watch that we had talked until three in the morning without a pause. The atmosphere in the room was now much lighter, and it gave me pleasure to talk to the investigators in Korean. But the pleasure felt hollow, because a soft but inexorable voice in the back of my head knew that I and my family were done for.

Two days after my confession I began to feel a little more normal. The agents played a great part in lifting my spirits. They included me in their conversations, and we exchanged observations about our different ways of life. The handsome agent who had questioned me in Chinese was named Nark Jong, and there was a younger man stationed with me named Seng Ju. The female agent was a small, pretty woman named Li Ok.

It had been Seoul that defeated me, but there was still a nagging doubt in the back of my mind. I had seen a lot of impressive buildings, a lot of suggestions of happiness. But what were the people of Seoul really like? Behind the facades of those impressive buildings and expensive things, were they really happy?

That day I asked Li Ok, "Could I see how ordinary people live here?"

"Of course, anytime," she replied, and conveyed my request to her superiors.

During my trips to Europe I felt as though I had not gleaned a complete picture of the life there. It was part of our directive that special agents were not allowed to speak to foreigners unless it was absolutely necessary. With the tension of our mission always looming overhead, it was impossible really to *experience* the countries we visited. Now, in Seoul, I wanted to do just that. In the past I could only make judgments about a country from superficial observations and from what I could discern from walking along a street. If I went to a market and found an abundance of goods, I would conclude that the country was better off than North Korea. If I saw a lot of bars and pubs, I assumed that the culture was decadent and immoral. If I saw beggars in the street, then the country was obviously destitute and couldn't feed its people.

Within a few minutes the preparations were made. Li Ok asked if there was anyplace in particular I wanted to see.

"No, I really wouldn't know," I replied. "Anywhere you like. Someplace . . . typical of Seoul."

Once outside, Li Ok walked next to me. Nark Jong walked behind us, Seng Ju just ahead. I was given twenty-five thousand won to spend—about twenty dollars—which seemed like an enormous amount of money.

We started in the narrow alleys of the Myung Dong district. We soon came upon a department store called Lotte's, and I was told that the name came from the German writer Goethe.

We walked inside. I was curious to see if the merchandise was foreign-made. The quality was excellent, but the names were foreign, and I pointed this out to Li Ok.

"No, they're made in Korea," she answered. "Most of these products are exported to other countries, which is why they have these labels. Anyway, why don't you buy something?"

I walked up to the cosmetics counter with some trepidation. The sales worker was a friendly woman whose courtesy was entirely alien to me. In the North, shop managers tend to be rude and brusque, since there's not much to be sold anyway. Here people seemed genuinely willing to help.

"Can I help you?" said the clerk.

I indicated a facial cream and tried not to stammer. "Is this imported?"

She picked up the bottle. "No, this is made by the Lucky Corporation here in Seoul. It's only sixty-five hundred won."

I had expected the cream to cost a fortune and was happy that I could afford it. It was impossible to gauge the true worth of my money, but I knew that the investigators wouldn't have given me too much. All the same, I was too timid to buy the cream. It was hard to get used to the free and easy atmosphere.

Li Ok bought me a scarf. I was bewildered by the variety of the merchandise and was afraid to choose anything for myself. Then we walked on. The streets were filled with people, but they did not seem to be in any hurry. Groups of men and women walked about freely, laughing among themselves. We ran into a man who was holding out a pot and ringing a bell, wearing some strange uniform. I thought that he must be some beggar, but Li Ok explained that he was collecting for the Salvation Army to help the poor.

"It's Christmas Eve," she said, urging me to make a donation. "It's a good time of year to be generous."

I was swept up by the high spirits of everyone but was still very confused. Christmas is not celebrated in the North, and most families have never heard of it. Why should the South, being a non-Western country, celebrate Christmas? Of course, being a puppet of the Yankee Imperialists was one explanation, but people seemed to be genuinely happy. They carried presents under their arms, and some were even caroling. I felt suddenly sad, as if I somehow was being excluded.

I was surprised to find the shopkeepers actually standing in front of their stores and vying for customers. It would be some time before I could understand that competition was the force that drove commerce here and was in fact the very reason why Seoul was so prosperous.

"I'm hungry," I said. "Can we get something to eat?"

"Of course," said Li Ok. She led me down a narrow alleyway that was lined with restaurants. Food was on display in the windows—mouth-watering displays of rice cakes, tempura, headcheese, blood sausages—even Chop Ciao, a Korean dish made of noodles, vegetables, and meat. I was astounded by the abundance and remembered that headcheese had not been available in the North for ten years. And my mother had considered herself lucky to come across a spoiled watermelon.

Oh, if only I could bring my family here. . . . It was so hard to think of their hardship when all this was spread before me.

"What would you like?" said Li Ok. "You can choose the place yourself."

Since blood sausages were a favorite of mine, I pointed to a small eatery that specialized in them. The place was crowded, and most people were drinking Soju, a traditional Korean rice liquor. We bought our food and took some seats. Next to us a group of middle-aged businessmen were complaining about the recent election.

"We can't just blame the government," said one. "You can't expect much when people think only of themselves."

"Personally I think if the minority parties had formed a coalition, they could have won the election."

I looked expectantly at my escorts, waiting for them to arrest these people who talked so freely and critically about their government. But the agents, if they had noticed, didn't seem to care. They were enjoying their food and seemed uninterested in anything else.

Later, on the way back to Namsan, when I was feeling more and more ill at ease in this outspoken society, I asked the investigators how anyone could so freely criticize the government.

They all laughed. "This is a democratic country," said Li Ok when she had recovered. "We have freedom of speech here. There's no law against criticizing the government."

"I don't understand," I replied, unimpressed by her reasoning. "It's hard to believe anything gets done at all in this country. But anyway, I was noticing something else. When we passed a construction site back there, I only saw a few workers. Where were they all? Do they work at night?"

"Well," said Nark Jong, who appeared puzzled by my question, "how do they do it in the North?"

"Everyone is mobilized," I said. "We get the army, the students, and the People's Councils together to dig, mix the cement, carrying the bricks—all in perfect order." I spoke with pride. It had always been a good feeling to be part of raising a building, and my people worked so hard.

"I see," he replied. "Nothing like that happens here. We have machines doing most of the work."

It came to me then that I couldn't hope to evaluate the technological advances of this country. It was like being on another planet. Why hadn't the North modernized its construction industry to this degree?

I had so many questions. I wondered if I would live long enough to have them answered.

A few days later we took a drive in the countryside, and visited Duksoo Palace. I had been told that the South Korean culture had been utterly supplanted by the Americans, but the palace was a well-preserved relic of Korean history. There was a statue in front of King Sejong, who invented the Korean alphabet. I was glad to be outside, but had not shaken the sense of depression and dread that had plagued me since the day after my confession. But I was delighted by the statue, because I knew nothing of the origins of the Korean alphabet.

We moved farther into the countryside and came upon a small village. Nothing appeared too different from a rural village in the North, although the winter landscape was rather lonely. Li Ok remarked, "This is Wondang. It's becoming popular among commuters because the air is so clean here."

We stopped the car in front of a sagging farmhouse. The yard had no gate, so we walked toward the front door and looked for signs of occupancy. There seemed to be no one around, and we went inside the house. I was surprised to find two refrigerators and a telephone in the kitchen. In the North rural life had no such comforts.

My companions, wholly absorbed with the farmhouse, were conversing among themselves. "This is very interesting," said Seng Ju. "Even out here, they've got all the amenities—electricity, television. It's not much like a farmhouse, if you ask me."

"You said it," agreed Nark Jong. "There's no romance out here anymore. We should all be sitting around a fire, roasting sweet potatoes."

"Still, did you notice that the door wasn't locked?" said Li Ok. "How many people in Seoul would leave their doors unlocked?"

We remained in the country for a while longer and then returned to Seoul. Li Ok suggested that we visit the East Gate Market, a vast collection of shops and restaurants. We entered a fabric shop, and right away I was surrounded by saleswomen making their pitches. They were cheerful and colorfully dressed, and I felt a bit flustered by their attentions. And then one of them said something that made my heart skip a beat.

"Wait a minute. Aren't you Kim Hyun Hee?"

There was a long silence. I felt my body go cold as other customers gathered around, whispering curiously.

"Who is she?"

"Kim Hyun Hee. You know, the one who blew up the airplane."

They became excited and pushed forward for a closer look. My escorts immediately moved in, guiding me out of the store before the situation got out of control. As we left, one of the saleswomen called, "Come back anytime, Hyun Hee. I'll give you any dress here for free!"

Although unnerved, I was not eager to return to Namsan, and suggested that we continue through the market. As we walked, I asked Li Ok, "You know, I haven't seen any shops here that sell nylon. Is it scarce here?" Privately I assumed that the South Koreans hadn't advanced to the level of making nylon, which was a North Korean luxury item.

"We don't really use nylon here," she replied as we threaded our way through the afternoon crowds. "It was discovered some time ago that it could be hazardous to one's health. We use cotton-based fibers now, which are just as durable. Nowadays nylon is considered low-quality material."

I was tempted to laugh. "This is unbelievable. Everything here is just the opposite of North Korea. Back there people couldn't afford to be concerned about their health. We were lucky to get nylon at all."

We proceeded to Joongbu Market, which specialized in dried fish. There were piles of squid, anchovies, seaweed, and the like. At the end of the market was an outdoor eatery, with just one long table and a bench on either side. Curious, I went closer. "What kind of people eat here?"

"Working-class, mainly," replied Li Ok. "Street merchants, dockworkers, truck drivers—that sort."

"Well, they're eating better than my family," I said, noting the rich variety of rice, noodles, headcheese, and Soojebie (a Korean soup made out of broken dough sheets) being sold. "Can we eat here?"

Li Ok looked at the other agents, who shook their heads. "We're too vulnerable here," said Nark Jong. "It would be easy for you to be recognized. I suggest we try a Nangmyun house nearby."

As we retraced our steps through the market, Li Ok explained that the Nangmyun (cold noodle soup) restaurants in this district were well known throughout Seoul. The first one we came upon must have been quite famous; there were expensive cars parked along the street and there was a line just to get in. We queued up, and the line seemed to be moving quickly enough. I was struck again by the simple, easygoing atmosphere of Seoul. The North seemed such a sterile place by comparison. There were fewer people, hardly any cars, and strangers never spoke to one another in the street. There was a basic lack of humor in day-to-day life. Seoul by comparison seemed so vibrant and full of energy.

After a few minutes we were admitted into the restaurant, and the hostess escorted us to a table in the corner. I was amazed by the place. There was no equivalent in the North. The restaurant was filled to capacity and bubbling with conversation, and waiters were rushing everywhere with platters of food. We all ordered Nangmyun and, when it came, began to eat ravenously.

A group of well-dressed men were seated at the table next to us, speaking in loud voices. It was impossible not to overhear what they were saying, so I listened to them idly as I ate.

"Think of Lee Woong Pyung," one of them was saying. "He made a fortune just for *defecting*."

"Well, the Soviet plane he flew here must have been worth some money. Still, the government must be spending a fortune on those defectors."

"Speaking of the North, did you see a picture of Kim Hyun Hee?"

"Yeah. A goddamn nymphomaniac, I'd bet, with a face like that. They say she can handle several men at once."

"That's why everyone feels such sympathy toward her, because of her looks. If she'd been some ugly little bitch, she'd have been executed already."

"You think she's a virgin?"

"Who knows. With a body like that I wouldn't bet on it."

My hand, paused halfway to my mouth, began to tremble. The noodles suspended from my chopsticks quivered comically. The agents, observing my distress, tried to calm me.

"Hey, it's okay, we shouldn't have come here," said Li Ok soothingly. "Come on, let's get out of here."

But I was too angry to be placated so easily. Slowly I placed the chopsticks on the table and picked up my soup bowl. I stood, turned to the men beside us, and threw the contents into their midst. They looked up, shocked. I was so furious that I couldn't contain myself.

"You sons of bitches," I said a low, cold voice. "Who the hell do you think you are talking about?"

"My God!" said one of them, looking up at me in astonishment. "It's her!"

"Yes, it's me," I snapped. "And you're lucky I don't beat the crap out of you right here and now."

They stared at me in stunned silence. By now we were attracting a lot of attention, and Li Ok was impelling me toward the door before I could react. The other agents covered our retreat, and Seng Ju left some money on the table. I was now embarrassed at all the whispering about me and the countless stares I was receiving and was grateful when we got outside.

Li Ok flagged the first taxi that passed, and we all piled in. Seng Ju looked out the back window for a time to see if we were being followed. "That one might make the papers," he remarked, scanning the streets behind us.

"I don't care," I replied angrily. "How could you let them say those awful things?"

Li Ok intervened, her voice soothing. "Hyun Hee, this isn't the North. We can't arrest people on the spot, no matter what they say. What were we supposed to do? You nearly caused a riot as it was."

The cab dropped us near the East Gate Market, where we'd left the car. As we drove back to Namsan, she said, "So how did you like our outing today? It was all right except for the last incident, wasn't it?"

"I'm not going out again," I replied, still terribly upset and on the verge of tears.

"Why? Because people recognized you? Because you're afraid of what they'll say about you?"

"Maybe," I said, wiping my eyes, "but it's a lot more than that. Every time we go out, it's great to feel the fresh air and walk around the city. But this world"—I waved my hand toward the window—"has nothing to do with me. These people have their own lives. I mean, what's the point of it all when I'm going to die soon anyway?" I broke down, sobbing miserably.

Li Ok tried to soothe me. "We can't control your fate, Hyun Hee. That's up to the courts. But in the meantime we can try to make you as happy as possible."

"I don't want to be happy," I answered. "I want you to kill me and have done with it."

There was worse to come in the days that followed. Li Ok told me one morning that on January 15 I would have to disclose my confession to the public at a press conference.

I was outraged. "Haven't I already told you everything? Why do I have to go through it all over again? Please, just kill me!"

"Listen," Nark Jong snapped. "It's not up to you or me whether you live or die. Is that clear? The only thing left for you is to repent your actions. If you feel sorry for the families of the

victims, you'll cooperate in any way that you can. In the meantime I don't want to hear any more of this 'kill me, kill me'
business. It's pathetic.''

I was chastened by his outburst, which was so unlike him.
Nark Jong, like Li Ok and Seng Ju, had showed me nothing but
kindness, and his words carried all the more weight for his
anger.

"Yes, I'm sorry," I replied quietly. "I'll do whatever I can."

January 15, 1988.

The investigators had worked for several days to prepare a
public statement divulging the results of their inquiry. The announcement was to be made in a lecture hall in the Bureau of
Security, and members of the press from all over the world
would be in attendance.

The morning was cold and rainy, and this did nothing to ease
my anxiety as we drove into the city. When we stopped in front
of the Security building, the car was surrounded by reporters.
Along with the three agents, two extra personal bodyguards
had been assigned to me, and there was a strong police presence.

The car door was thrown open, and I was guided through
the crowd. I was jostled and nearly pushed over, and everyone
seemed to be calling my name. Cameras were clicking furiously. My guards cleared a path for me into the building, and
somehow we made it inside. At that point Li Ok and another
female agent locked their arms in mine, and Nark Jong took a
position just behind me.

As we entered the lecture hall, I was blinded by a furry of
flashbulbs. I was momentarily dazed and again had to be
pushed forward. I was escorted to a chair in the front of the
room and told to look up. The flashbulbs erupted again, and I
was forced to look down.

It is impossible to remember the details of the press conference. I was asked question after question, which I answered as
best I could. I withheld nothing, though I of course was con-
stantly oppressed by the thought that my family was surely
done for now that my confession was public. When the con-

ference was over, I felt numb and was glad to return to the peace of Namsan.

The investigators tried to revive my spirits a few days later with a trip to South Seoul Park. To my surprise I thoroughly enjoyed myself. South Seoul is an amusement park with all sorts of rides, and as I was thrown and knocked about, I laughed and screamed with joy. It brought me completely out of my depression, and for a few short hours I was living only in the moment. I felt rather infantile for shrieking the way I did, but it was one of the few moments in my life where I actually had fun.

The investigators were pleased with my change of mood. Since the press conference they had been even more courteous and helpful and had brought a television into my room. The variety and depth of the news coverage was astounding, and I paid close attention, since I was usually featured. Every now and then the newscasters would report something utterly untrue or exaggerate insignificant details all out of proportion. I would furiously complain to Li Ok about this, who would try to calm me down.

"Hyun Hee, you just have to ignore it," she said. "You can't control everything that is said about you. Anyway, the coverage in the North is probably far worse, isn't it?"

"Maybe," I retorted. "But in the North at least they don't carry any defamatory stories attacking people."

"No, I suppose they don't," said Nark Jong, chiming in. "They just arrest you and have done with it."

"Or shoot you," offered Seng Ju.

Whenever I heard statements like this, I immediately, by sheer reflex, became defensive. Though Seoul had won me over, I could not overcome a lifetime of conditioning so quickly, and I found myself irritated with their snide remarks.

"Look at Kim Il Sung," said Seng Ju one day. "I mean, the bastard's ancient, but he still won't kick the bucket."

"Well, they say that the bad guys always live longer," said Nark Jong.

"It's not his fault," I snapped. "It's just that his subordinates misguide him or don't follow his directions properly."

This sent them into hysterics, and I felt my blood boiling. But the worst occasions were when the agents castigated the North Koreans as a whole. This saddened me deeply. I wanted to point out that North Koreans were real flesh-and-blood people. It seemed terrible that there was so much ignorance on both sides, and a national tragedy that people of the same heritage were so divided. We had the same language, the same customs, and the same common history, and yet we were at each other's throats.

But any attachments I still harbored toward the North vanished one morning as I watched the news. In recent days there had been stories about my presenting flowers to a South Korean delegation as a child, along with some photographs of the incident. I remembered the occasion well. But the North had just released a videotape of a woman named Chung Hee Sun, who claimed that *she* had been the girl who presented the flowers to the South Koreans. Venomously she declared that the South Koreans were only spreading propaganda by saying that I was the same girl.

But that was not the worst of it. South Korea had correctly stated that I, the girl in the picture, had grown up to destroy an airplane. Operating on the ploy that this was indeed true, Hee Sun, in a typical example of North Korean doublespeak, went on to say that the South Koreans were attempting to frame *her* for the plane crash. In other words, since she was the girl in the picture, and since the girl and the terrorist were the same person, how could *she* have gone on to destroy an airplane when she was only a middle school teacher in Pyongyang? The average North Korean, after witnessing this well-rehearsed act, would conclude that his or her country had had absolutely nothing to do with the bombing and that South Korea was trying to frame the North. And because my name was never mentioned, I was no more than a fictional character created by the South Koreans to serve this purpose.

I watched the television in shock. My country, for whom I had killed 115 people and nearly died myself, had turned its back on me. First they had used me. Now they had abandoned me. I felt an enormous sense of emptiness. I was too stunned to feel angry and could only shake my head at the screen.

"What do you think of that?" I said, almost to myself.

"What do I think of what?" said Li Ok.

"That woman."

"Her? Just a typical North Korean tactic."

"Do you think she looks like me?"

"She does resemble the flower girl in that photograph, though she doesn't look much like you now. Keep in mind, though, that she was carefully chosen for that resemblance. It's pure propaganda."

"Those bastards," I said, almost whispering, as I stared at the TV. "Shouldn't we broadcast a denial?"

"Absolutely not. That's what they're expecting. They're trying to distract attention from the bombing by focusing on something immaterial. They've been pushed into a corner, you see, and are trying to find a way out of it. The best policy is to ignore it. You'll see."

I cannot describe the sense of betrayal I felt. It seemed as though I had lived twenty-six years for nothing. And indeed in North Korea I no longer existed. I had become an *unperson.* And my family would become *unpeople.*

I would never forget my family, nor give up hope that they would be spared their lives. At the same time, however, I could not go on thinking of myself as a North Korean, not if the rebirth I had experienced after taking the poison was to be complete. I would have to let go of my childhood, my years in college, indeed my whole life until the moment I had collapsed in the Bahrain airport. And though I did so with tremendous grief, I nevertheless felt a surge of excitement when I spoke the words "Kim Hyun Hee, South Korean."

CHAPTER SIXTEEN

I HAD THOUGHT that once I confessed, everything would become much easier and that I would be quickly executed. But one day, about a week later, Nark Jong said that I would soon be facing trial, where my fate would be decided.

"Trial?" I demanded. "I've told you everything! I'm guilty! What could there possibly be left to discuss?"

"I'm afraid it's unavoidable," he replied. "You should be thankful that you haven't been shot already, as you would have been in the North. In South Korea everyone charged with a crime is entitled to a fair trial to determine their guilt or innocence and to be sentenced accordingly. It's what we call justice."

"Well, I call it ridiculous. It seems like a complete waste of time, given the fact I've admitted everything."

My situation appeared unlikely to change soon, and I resigned myself to a long stay in Namsan. Later that day I was reading through one of Nark Jong's reports, which he had left in the room. Most of it described my behavior since I had arrived at Namsan, and the details of his investigation. But when I came to the section marked "Opinion," however, I sat up in my seat and felt myself going cold.

> There being sufficient evidence of Kim Hyun Hee's guilt to support a conviction on each and every charge, I am of the opinion that the punishment under consideration is entirely appropriate.

You bastard, I thought. *You lying, filthy bastard.* I now felt doubly betrayed, and within moments I was sobbing. Why should Nark Jong be so nice to me, only to recommend that I be executed? Had his sympathy over the past few weeks been nothing but a charade?

I cried for a long time. I felt utterly alone. I despaired because no matter how nice the agents appeared to be, there were some incontrovertible facts underlying it all—I was a murderer, and murderers are executed. All the pleasantries meant nothing. Each day we went into Seoul to shop or look around was only a tantalizing glimpse of a life I would never be allowed to lead. But what hurt the most was that I thought that Nark Jong was on my side. I thought he of all people understood my pain and would support me. Apparently I had been wrong.

As it happened, the trial did not start for another year, on March 7, 1989. The months in between went slowly. After I read Nark Jong's recommendation, I refused to talk to any of the agents or leave my room for weeks. They were concerned about the change in my character and sent for a doctor to look me over. He found nothing wrong with me except my persistent depression, which was natural considering the circumstances. I passed the time watching TV and reading newspapers. I also read Western books that the agents brought in. But it was a joyless existence. I had been reborn in Seoul, but I was nothing more than an orphan.

When the trial finally came, it proceeded very quickly. There was no need for a jury, since I was pleading guilty to every charge brought against me. I was forced to repeat everything I had told the agents in my confession, but the whole incident was little more than a formality. My sentencing was set for March 27, and as I have indicated, I received the death penalty.

An execution date was not immediately set, so I was obliged to return to Namsan and wait yet again. Now that death was a certainty, I could never shake it from my mind. I spent entire days just gazing up at the white ceiling. It is one thing to want death, it is another to be told that it will indeed soon happen. My new life in Seoul was evidently going to be a very short one. I had been reborn, and I had seen glimpses of what my new life might have been like. But now only cold death awaited.

I paid little attention to the editorials in the newspapers speculating about possible clemency from the government. The families of the victims were vocal in their demands that I not be pardoned, and who could blame them? No one could restore their lost relatives to them, and the only vindicating consequence, unsatisfactory though it might be, would be my death. Only that catharsis could allow them to continue with some measure of peace in their lives.

Each day felt meaningless, a mere exercise in futility. I learned that the sentence would be carried out within six months, which at least gave me some estimate of what time remained. I sank into a deep depression and refused to talk to the agents. I told myself that I should have been dead in Bahrain anyway and that my new life was nothing more than a fluke. And yet everyone, by sheer instinct, clings to life. It's what our bodies tell us to do, and we cannot ignore it. I was afraid.

We have all in our lives seen others in distress, and while sympathetic, we are glad that it is they, and not we, who are suffering. People are injured, or contract diseases, and sometimes die; and it is they who must pay the awful price; it is always someone else. But this time it was me. This time others would look on, safely, while I was put to death.

Nark Jong, strangely enough, remarked one day that he hoped I would be pardoned. I wondered if he had recommended my execution from a purely judicial standpoint and had known all along that a pardon was inevitable. Maybe the sentence was nothing but a formality; maybe it was the president's province, and not that of the judge, to grant clemency. Or perhaps Nark Jong had just changed his mind. But either way it was a great relief to sense that his feelings were genuine.

Later that day Li Ok was in my room, talking to her mother at home. She was gossiping in a carefree way, as though without a concern in the world, and I envied her so much. If I had only been South Korean, I might at this moment be calling my own mother, perhaps from my own house, with a husband and children in the background. All I wanted was something that had been denied me all along—to live an ordinary life.

I recalled that my mother had said she cried every night after I was recruited into the Party. She told me she would take out my picture and cry herself to sleep. This was strictly forbidden; the moment I became a special agent, she was to have destroyed all photographs of me. But she could not. And my sister would tell me that she was secretly hoping that I could one day be married.

If only my mother knew the truth. I wondered if she could ever believe it.

One thing happened during this period that was a major change in my behavior: I began to pray to God. Western religion was not uncommon in Korea, and I had picked up bits and pieces from books, television, and conversations around me. I prayed to God that I could atone for my sins. I prayed for a chance to live so that I could serve others. Without the support of these prayers I might have lost hope entirely.

Spring was on its way, but while the rest of the city was anticipating the end to the long winter, I was stuck in my damp, cold dungeon. Waiting.

CHAPTER SEVENTEEN

APRIL CAME TO SEOUL, and spring breathed into every crevice. The hills around Namsan were covered with the red, pink, and yellow blossoms of azaleas and forsythias. The magnificent cherry blossoms seemed to defy the fact that winter had ever existed. Seoul was coming to life.

Rumors of a pardon grew, and I rose out of my depression somewhat into a state of fretful anticipation. Despite my reticence, the agents still volunteered to take me outside every now and then. With spring in the air it was impossible not to accept.

So I basked in the warm sunshine and gazed at the beautiful countryside around me. South Korea, like the North, is a breathtaking country. There are lush valleys, high mountains, fertile plains. I hoped that I could one day experience all its beauties for myself.

Back at Namsan I kicked off my shoes and turned on the seven o'clock news. "Another day lost," I said to Li Ok, who would be on duty for another two hours. But she didn't answer. She was staring at the TV.

"The government granted a pardon today to Kim Hyun Hee,

convicted recently of the bombing of Korean Air Flight Eight-fifty-eight. The president said that Kim Hyun Hee was not the true culprit in the bombing but instead only an innocent victim of a society that continues to lack any respect for human rights and is ruled by a reign of terror. According to the president, it is Kim Il Sung who should . . ."

But I heard nothing more. At that moment Li Ok jumped into the air and screamed: "IT'S A PARDON!!"

She rushed over to hug me, pounding my back. Soon the news had spread throughout Namsan, and everyone stopped by to congratulate me. They all seemed genuinely happy, not least Nark Jong.

I was too overwhelmed to speak, and while everyone was buzzing with delight and discussing the details of the president's decision, I slipped over to my bed and began to cry. I cannot describe the flux of emotions I felt—gratitude toward the government, grief for my family, hope for the future. It seemed that my loneliness was as great as my joy, but that did not stop me from offering a prayer on the spot.

Thank you, God, for giving a new charter of life to this sinner. Please give this news to my parents, and show your mercy to them as well.

Nark Jong wandered over to me, smiling. He seemed amazed that I was crying, but I think that he sensed my complex emotional state and didn't want to pry too far.

"It's a happy day, Hyun Hee. It's time that you plan a new life, here in Seoul. I'll stop by tomorrow and we'll talk about it."

I nodded, his face blurred from my tears. "Thank you *so* much. I thought you had turned against me."

He seemed abashed, and it was a moment before he replied. "It's been a difficult time for all of us, Hyun Hee. We haven't had this kind of episode in a long time. I must admit that I had to wrestle with my own conscience and emotions. But this was never a black-and-white issue, you know. And part of the president's decision was probably based on political reasons and not just moral ones. You're an excellent example of the tragedy that is North Korea, and that's not going to be lost on anybody.

"Nevertheless I think there would be little point in executing you. It won't bring back the victims and it won't punish the real villains, who are Kim Il Sung and Kim Jung Il. You never had a chance in that society, Hyun Hee, and I think it would be a terrible waste of human life just to kill you off. It won't solve anything, and I know that you truly regret what you did. Besides, I don't think you pose any danger to our society." He smiled. "Despite all your training, I don't think there's a criminal bone in your body. I think any one of us would have done the same in your shoes."

"Yes, I think so too," said Li Ok, who had joined the conversation and taken my hand in her own. "You know, I think a foreigner might not understand this decision. I think one has to have lived through the painful division of Korea to appreciate it. People elsewhere couldn't imagine what it's like to have their country split in two, with one half ruled by a cruel tyrant. Many of us have relatives in North Korea whom we've never seen. You never know. Maybe this awful mission of yours will help us unify after all.

"Anyway, what's important now is the pardon, Hyun Hee. You're a free woman now."

CHAPTER EIGHTEEN

LIKE THE BRIGHT morning that returns after a long dark night, there was a morning in my life too. I was in a new room, with windows, and the morning sunlight was dazzling. I opened the window to let in the fresh spring air. There was a deep valley outside the window, which sloped up to a mountain on the other side. The flowers that covered the hills seemed all the more brilliant on this morning.

There was a group of mountain climbers scaling the heights in the distance, and I could hear their voices carried across the valley. I felt the urge to call out to them, but I didn't want to disturb Li Ok, who was sleeping nearby.

The morning newspaper had been slid under the door. I unfolded it to the front page. KIM HYUN HEE PARDONED, stated the bold letters. I was deeply glad to see those words because it confirmed absolutely that the news was true. But I was afraid to read the article.

We went into Seoul that day to Grand Park, which was filled with students and tourist groups. On this day I was happy to mingle with the crowd. I felt that I was no longer an alien. I belonged. It felt incredibly good.

A group of schoolgirls were playing Handkerchief Tag, the Korean equivalent of Duck Duck Goose. I watched them enviously for a moment and said to Li Ok, "You know, I used to play that game myself." And it was much more fun than the games we learned later, after Kim Jung Il had banned it, where we would sing things like "Forward, forward we march, to crush the Americans."

We moved on to an art museum. As one might suspect, it was far different from the museums I had been used to in North Korea. For one thing, half of the art seemed based around the naked body, which was taboo in the North. It brought to mind a movie that we special agents had been shown back in training camp called *It's a Dog-Eat-Dog Society!* It was a documentary intended to show the perverse decadence of Western culture, and it showed artists covering themselves with paints and rolling naked over their canvases. During such scenes we were required to say, "It really is a dog's world."

The art in the museum, however, was diverse and more refined. Li Ok and the others soon tired and had to wait on benches while I roamed happily about for another three hours. I felt like skipping.

Gradually a new life of sorts began to take shape. Although I was technically "free," I would have to remain for some time at Namsan. The Intelligence grapevine had it that North Korean agents in Seoul had orders to assassinate me and that my life would be in danger if I remained unguarded. I really didn't mind. I had a new room, a TV, and the continued company of Nark Jong, Seng Ju, and Li Ok. I also began to study theology with a Reverend Han, who had seen me occasionally during my trial and taught me some Bible verses.

"You've been granted a new lease on life," he said one day as we walked along the hillside near Namsan, with the agents a few paces behind to guard us. "Why don't you give a confession of faith to my congregation? We'd be glad to have you."

"Oh, I couldn't, Reverend," I answered, feeling embarrassed. "I don't deserve to. I may have been pardoned, but we both know that I'm a sinner."

"We're all sinners, Hyun Hee. Moreover, I think you're living proof of God's miracles, if you want to know the truth."

"But how do I give this . . . confession?"

"You simply tell the congregation that you're returning thanks to the Lord who has shown you his grace. Tell them about your conversion to Christianity and your belief in God's grace. It's really very easy."

I thought about it as we walked. Religion, as I have mentioned, had been scorned and ridiculed in the North. But I knew that the Bible passages Reverend Han had shown me made a great deal of sense, at least to me. I knew enough that Christianity was an article of faith and not science; but the Scriptures really touched my heart, even as a non-Westerner. I began to see evidence of God's works in everything around me, and I felt comfortable calling myself a Christian.

All the same, I didn't feel worthy of God's love at times, and in any event I was afraid to speak before an audience under any circumstances. But Reverend Han had been good to me. He had never judged me and he had always given me a measure of hope. With some trepidation I agreed to the confession.

He was delighted, and we set a date for May 16. When that day came, Li Ok went out and bought me a fashionable two-piece suit, which I hesitated to wear because of its short skirt. I had been called beautiful by many people during my life, but I had never believed it to be true. I had never had much confidence in my sexuality, since for most of my life it had been rigorously suppressed. The whole realm of physical attraction was completely mysterious to me.

But at Li Ok's urging I put on the suit anyway. Nark Jong walked in when I was dressed and seemed flabbergasted when he saw me.

"You're making this young man dizzy," he joked. I smiled. Nark Jong was fifty, handsome, and unmarried, although I didn't know much more beyond that. His words made me both proud and shy, and I couldn't think of anything to say in reply.

We left for the church. The traffic was heavy, and we barely made it there on time. Reverend Han told me to wait in an anteroom while he introduced me and gave me a few last words of encouragement before walking out to the pulpit.

When at last I was introduced, I was greeted by a warm round of applause, which utterly surprised me. There were plenty of reporters present, but for some reason I didn't feel uncomfortable. I stood at the lectern, my throat dry, and gave

177

a few brave coughs. At length I found my voice and began. "Hello."

I listened to my voice reverberate through the church, and I felt suddenly larger than life.

"The Lord has shown me his great works and miracles," I began, and proceeded to recite the speech I had prepared. When I was finished, there was a chorus of "Amens," and many of the parishioners were crying. It was overwhelming to me that I should be shown such forgiveness, and I was thankful that I had found this sanctuary of God to help me in my new life.

Perhaps the most shocking—and joyous—incident since my arrest occurred a few days later. Nark Jong rushed into my room during the evening as I was watching the sky turn crimson in the sunset and enjoying the evening breeze on my face. The sunlight cast a warm glow on the blooming hillside, and I was feeling glad simply to be alive to see this scene.

"Look at this," he said, thrusting a photograph at me. "Recognize anyone?"

I scanned the black-and-white photograph and went numb. "My God. Where did you get this?"

"So you do," he prodded.

"Of course," I said. It was a photograph of my mother's class in middle school, the same one that she had shown me years ago. Her image immediately stood out to me, and I felt as though I were being reunited with her. I felt tears come to my eyes. How I missed her! "How did you get this?" I asked again, shaken.

"Ah," he said, grinning. "That's a good story. It seems, Miss Kim, that you have relatives in Seoul."

July 21, 1989.

A meeting had been arranged at the Five Northern Provinces Administration Hall. There would be many reporters in attendance, but I didn't care. They had found a man named Im Kwan Ho, who was purportedly a cousin of my mother's father.

My heart fluttered in anticipation as we arrived. Inside the hall, in a large conference room, I stepped through a crowd of reporters, hardly noticing them, ignoring their questions. My eyes were fixed ahead.

And then I saw him. I thought for a moment that I was looking at my Uncle Kwan Shik, my grandfather's brother. He noticed me and waved, but apparently we were not allowed to speak to each other yet. There were policemen present and they wanted to confirm that he was indeed my relative. We were asked a few biographical questions, but I needed no more proof. He looked *exactly* like Kwang Shik.

When the formalities had been dispensed with, I rushed forward and hugged him. "Uncle, why did you seek me out?" I blubbered through my tears. "You didn't have to, you know. Why should you subject yourself to all this awful publicity?"

He, too, was crying, but when I said this, he laughed. "How could I not?" he said.

We were led to another room where we could be free of the reporters. Kwan Ho introduced me to his sister and children, who were waiting for us inside. When everyone had been introduced, we all sat down. Kwan Ho began his story.

"Your grandfather, Hyun Hee, was an accomplished calligrapher and one of the wealthiest men in Gaesung. His house had seventy rooms. Gaesung, as you know, became absorbed by North Korea after the war, and of course your father's fortune was stripped away. But some of us escaped to the South.

"Anyway, your mother, who by the way was an extraordinary dancer, attended a Christian school called Houston Girls' High School. The picture you were shown belongs to Mrs. Kim Bong Sook, who was a classmate of your mother's."

I was astounded to hear all this. But, it made perfect sense that my mother had kept it from me. Everything he had just said was anathema to the North Korean government—Christianity, wealth, an escape to the South. But I was touched to learn of my mother's Christianity. Once, when I was very young, I had contracted polio, from which I miraculously recovered. My mother walked around for days afterward saying, "God must have helped her" and "God has been good to us." I knew now that she had meant it.

We talked for hours about each other's backgrounds. They

were delighted to hear about my parents and my siblings, and I was overjoyed to know that I had relatives in my adopted (and adoptive) country. But of course a darker issue overshadowed the meeting—the fact that the rest of my family was still in the North, in the grip of tyranny.

On that day I made the resolution that my newfound freedom must serve the highest purpose possible. I would speak out whenever possible against Kim Il Sung and Kim Jung Il. I would do anything in my power to hasten the reunification of Korea—but this time from the other side. I would give speeches and interviews exposing the truth about North Korea and the men who rule it. I had been to many countries—Russia, Hungary, Austria, Italy, China, and more. And never once did I find a country whose people lived worse than the North Koreans.

Kim Il Sung and his family have done nothing less than rape the North Korean people of their culture and their right to lives of liberty and happiness. They have divided a nation and caused irreparable damage to its people. It is a tragedy of truly epic proportions.

And so in Seoul, where I was reborn, I sat with my own flesh and blood. There were tears of grief and tears of joy. For although we had at last come together, we were still incomplete. We could not rest easy until the breach between North and South was at last sealed. We could only work and hope for the day when our families, and indeed all Koreans, would again be as one.

EPILOGUE

DEAR FATHER, DEAR MOTHER:

This is Hyun Hee. Yes, I am alive and well, though it is hard to believe.

You probably recognized me just from seeing this handwriting. I can imagine how surprised you will feel if and when you read this letter.

It's been three years since we last parted. I have spent every day in tears just thinking about you all.

More than a few times I have woken up in tears after seeing you in my dreams, devastated that I was not really with you.

Mother and Father, I know I have not been a good eldest daughter to our family. I have made so many mistakes. After we last parted, when I was stationed in Guangzhou, China, I was given a secret mission of the greatest importance to our country. For this reason I was never able to visit you. I was not even allowed to walk beyond the front yard of our camp.

You see, in the years after I was recruited into the Party, I was trained to become field agent for the Bureau of Investigation. My assignments took me all over the world. And after I was stationed in Guangzhou, I was given the task of destroying

181

a Korean airplane. The goal was to deter the 1988 Olympics from being held in Seoul and to unify our country again. As you know, neither happened.

Instead the mission, which I had been led to believe was of profound importance to our fatherland, has left me with the deepest shame and mortal regret. For one thing about my mission did succeed: The plane blew up, and 115 people died.

I was captured a few days later by South Korean agents and extradited to Seoul. Here I confessed, was tried, and was sentenced to death.

Miraculously I have just learned that I have been granted a pardon. I am now, as it is said, a "free woman."

How can I explain all this to you? How can I explain that everything I ever learned in the North was false? South Korea is a beautiful country and can now compete economically with America, Japan, and Europe. And no matter how hard I try, I could never explain the magnitude of the progress that has occurred here. An ordinary household here has a color television, a video recorder, a phone, a refrigerator, and many even have cars.

It would also be difficult to find a family that has to worry about eating three meals a day, as in the North.

The people here have such freedom that at first I was not able to understand how a country could be managed with so many different opinions and ideas. And yet somehow it works.

I have heard Russian tourists say that South Korea is a paradise on Earth. And everyone here desires the reunification of our land and people. I myself was so committed to this ideal that I was misled into a morbid and twisted cause, and for the rest of my life will live with the blood of 115 lives on my hands.

People here have been very understanding, saying, "It is not your fault alone. Kim Il Sung and Kim Jung Il, who ordered you to commit the crime, must take responsibility." Well, there's nothing I can do to bring back the dead to their loved ones, but people's kindness here has helped me understand that I am not, after all is said and done, a heartless monster.

I recently read of a man named Kim Man Chul who escaped the North with his family by boat and crossed the 38th Parallel. I envy him, and wish that you could be here as well.

I have a surprise for you, Mother. I have met your relatives.

EPILOGUE

Not long ago I met your uncle, Im Kwan Ho, and also Hwang In Sook, Hwang Moon Sook, Hwang Young Sook, and Kim Bong Sook. They greeted me like their own family, and I see them often now. It helps to ease my loneliness, and I know that they are anxious to see you.

Now that the two parts of Germany have been reunited, I truly hope that our time, too, is not far away. And when that happens, I will be so glad to see you, and once again we can become a family. For there is a shining star behind the dark clouds, and there are living things that yearn to spring up from the frozen ground. We cannot give up hope.

I have a thousand things to say, but I will stop for now. I miss you so much.

Longing for you from Seoul,

Your Eldest Daughter,
Kim Hyun Hee
May 1991